CW01645803

DELIVEROO: THE OTHER SIDE OF THE RIDE

DELIVEROO: THE OTHER SIDE OF THE RIDE

BY

Owen Pickles

(Rider 496451)

WITH A FOREWORD BY

Josiah Shields

(Rider 536829)

Contents

Foreword

You may expect to read in the following pages and chapters a novel about life as a Deliveroo rider, about the process of couriering food from restaurant to customer and the challenges involved in such an occupation. You have, after all, been promised a look into 'the other side of the ride' – the part that you, the customer, do not see when you briefly open your door to receive the brown paper bag which contains your Deliveroo order. Fear not, for this does make up a large part of what you are about to read! However, as you progress through this book you are sure to begin to realise that it is more than just the story of an individual Deliveroo rider.

Pretty much anybody can become a Deliveroo rider – in fact the hardest part of the application is getting to the front of the waiting list for your local area! Thus, as I heard first-hand the accounts of Owen's Deliveroo exploits, I became inclined to give it a go for myself; I had a bike, a phone, and the ability to watch ten minutes of training videos and so there was really no reason not to. Thanks to a detailed rundown by Owen of how the whole system worked, I set off on my first shift feeling largely prepared and somewhat excited.

After I'd got a few deliveries under my belt, however, I started to realise that my experience was far removed from what I had been expecting. In a word, it was mundane. The only change in circumstances between Owen and myself was the location in which we were riding – he in London and I in our local town of Didcot – and yet this single alteration made the same job feel worlds apart. For a start, simply moving around in Didcot was far easier than in London – most of the housing estates have footpaths and shortcuts which oftentimes make cycling just as fast and easy as driving whilst also giving one a break from the car fumes and inconsiderate van drivers who fill England's roads. Far from the hectic carriageways of London, my experience of cycling in Didcot was actually quite enjoyable.

Another immediately noticeable difference between my time riding and Owen's was in the deliveries themselves. In Didcot every order originates from one of about ten vendors all located within a few hundred metres of each other, meaning that each delivery follows a more or less identical formula: 1) pick up the order from the town centre; 2) cycle about a mile to one of three housing estates; 3) knock on a door in a row of terraced new-builds; 4) hand over the food to a perfectly plain, ordinary individual. There was no drama, no peril; it was all very… normal. Thus, whilst the process of delivering food in Didcot was the same as in London, the actual experience of doing so was entirely different.

This is because 'the other side of the ride' is not the process of ferrying bags from one location to another. Rather, 'the other side of the ride' is the situations and characters whom one encounters upon the way, and who ultimately make the job of the Deliveroo rider a unique one.

This book is therefore as much a tour of the nation's capital from the unique perspective of a food courier – a profession with almost unrivalled access to both the highest and lowest realms of society – as it is the story of delivering food. It provides a glance into the bizarre, wacky, strange, and ultimately unique events and characters who fill the streets of London, and the one connection shared by all of them – a desire for food delivered directly to their doors.

Josiah Shields: Rider 536829

September 2022

Author's Note

All customers' names and addresses have been changed. If a customer's address corresponds to a real place, or a name to a real person, the link is purely coincidental. Nevertheless, I have tried as far as possible to recreate the impressions conveyed by names and addresses. The 'rider numbers' of Owen Pickles and Josiah Shields have also been changed to protect the security of their accounts. Any similarity to the numbers of other riders is purely coincidental.

There's not too much to get to grips with terminology-wise but, to save clogging up the story with definitions, 'stacked orders' are when a rider collects more than one order at once. They are a great way of earning more money quickly as the rider can go straight from customer to customer without having to return to the restaurant.

Furthermore, the theory is that, at the restaurant, the rider checks the contents of the package against a list of what it should contain. The practice, on the other hand, is that the rider grabs the package, shoves it into their bag, and gets on their way. This might seem like breaking the rules but if it is, it should be understandable when you consider that the order is usually in a sealed package and that if the seal is broken, the contents are likely to spill all over the rider's bag.

Finally, riders used to be paid a flat hourly rate with a bonus for every order completed – although there was an incentive to complete as many orders as possible, they would still be paid if they had to wait. Now, however, riders are paid per order so if they are waiting, they are losing money. On the other hand, if they do have an order, they are always in a massive rush to get it done and onto the next one to cram as many as possible in and thus earn as much money as possible.

O.P.

September 2022

Introduction: Solving a Problem

Only one thing could save me: early election to Parliament.

Fitzroy Maclean

In January 2021 it was the third English lockdown, my second term at university, and the first time in my life that I'd been thoroughly miserable. I was living alone in London, supposedly reading Law at King's College London but in fact reading Law on my laptop in my bedroom.

I was at university for one reason alone: ever since independently studying GCSE Law in Year 10, my ambition had been to become a barrister. I had this goal for three reasons: I liked law; I liked debating; and I liked wigs – and as far as I was aware, there was only one job on the planet that could satisfy all three of those desires. Unfortunately, it wasn't the sort of job one could just apply for straight out of school: the number of steps required to get there would, it seemed, constitute a good-sized ladder. As it was fairly obvious that one of those steps would be a degree, I had applied for and managed to get a place at King's College – which explained my arrival in London in September 2020, fresh-faced, eager, and gloriously independent.

On my arrival I had not done any academic work since my A-Levels had been cancelled some six months before. This had been good news at the time – I had intended to start revising the week that exams were cancelled, meaning that I hadn't done any unnecessary work. Now I could sit back, relax, and wait for my teachers to give me the grades I needed. Six months later, though, my mind was desperate for stimulation. As I started studying again, my liking for the law rapidly blossomed into a passion as I was able to embrace its nitty-gritty details and beautiful little foibles in their entirety.

There was only one small cloud on my bright horizon: due to government restrictions, my course was wholly online. This, however, was thankfully almost entirely offset by the generosity of the university in allowing me to book two three-hour slots at the library every week. When added to the fact that I was still rejoicing in my new-found independence, there was no doubt about it: overall, I was happy.

However, as the months passed the novelties began to fade and when I came back after Christmas, they had completely worn off. The library was completely closed; the September sun had been replaced by the dismal drizzle of January; and not even the intricacies of the law could comfort me. As no-one else in my (online) tutorials could be bothered to turn on their cameras or respond to questions, the classes usually resulted in me regurgitating the facts from the lectures to my tutor plus a load of initials. It was not an inspirational atmosphere. The prospect of becoming a barrister was a long way off.

By the end of the first week back I was bored stiff, lonely, and in need of money. To my view, there were two options: I could go home and cancel my tenancy agreement – giving me company and things to do, as well as reducing the flow of finance from my bank account – or I could sign up as a Deliveroo rider. The pros of the latter choice were obvious: it would entail having to spend hours cycling around the death-trap that London is pleased to call its roads; venturing outside in all weathers; and working an awful lot of hours to cover my costs. Meanwhile, I would still be living and studying alone. Given these factors, my conclusion was obvious. I would become a Deliveroo rider.

Admittedly there were one or two other considerations which influenced my decision. Primary in this regard was my desire, having spent the last few years working part-time as a butcher and poultry keeper, to complete my involvement in the food chain. I wanted to be able to claim that I had followed chickens from when they were hatched and reared, through being cut up, to when they were finally handed to a customer as part of a KFC. Whilst I doubted that such an achievement would merit a place in the Guinness World Records, it would at least allow me to see a new side to my previous activities.

With the above factors in mind, I did my research. It's difficult to think of a job that would be easier to get; to apply, all I had to do was click a link. If only it was that easy to become a barrister: no CV, no covering letter, no GCSEs, no A-Levels, no degree, no Bar Course, no pupillage… You might say that being a barrister is far more prestigious than being a Deliveroo rider and thus requires more qualifications. Not having become a barrister yet, I can't form a judgment on that. All I can say is that long since stopping riding, I continue to wear my Deliveroo T-shirt as a badge of achievement.

I did have a slight suspicion that I wouldn't exactly fit in with the other riders in my area: from what I had seen most of them were immigrant men with very limited English, whereas I hailed from a middle-class village in south Oxfordshire and had achieved top grades in my English GCSEs. Those of my acquaintances more disposed to be pleasant had on occasion described me as well-spoken, well-dressed, and well-connected. On the other hand, those less disposed to be pleasant had described me as a deliberate eccentric, and it's fair to say my time at sixth form hadn't altogether dispelled that impression. I was used to not fitting in. That would not be a problem.

All doubts were therefore resolved so I submitted my application and a couple of days later found myself signing an employment contract like no other. It stated that: (a) it was not an employment contract; (b) a percentage of my earnings would go to Deliveroo (who was not my employer); and (c) I was free to use my Deliveroo kit to work for any of Deliveroo's competitors and use kit from any of Deliveroo's competitors to work for Deliveroo, although (d) I wouldn't actually be working *for* Deliveroo, as I was self-employed. Furthermore, (e) despite being self-employed, I was strongly advised to wear my Deliveroo kit as this would make me a walking, talking advert for Deliveroo (not the official language), which would get Deliveroo more custom and thus more work for its self-employed (non) employees. Though finally, (f) I did not have to do any work at all if I didn't want to. With that level of clarity, I didn't need to ask any questions. I signed the form unhesitatingly.

Now that I was on-board (although officially no more an employee than I had been the day before) the next step was to learn how to do the job. This was even less challenging than signing the contract as I didn't have to read anything. All I had to do was watch two five-minute videos explaining how the job worked. A summary of the videos was as follows:

1. One would download the Rider app onto one's phone.
2. Once downloaded, one would open it and click 'Go Online'. This (unsurprisingly) would take one online.
3. The software, chattily named 'Frank', would then assign one to an order based on factors such as one's proximity to the restaurant.
4. Frank would then give one a choice as to whether to accept the order (this was, presumably, where part (f) of the contract came in).

5. Having accepted the order (as self-employed people can't earn money by doing nothing), one would be provided with a route to the restaurant, which one would follow.
6. On arrival, one would be given an order number which one would show to someone in the restaurant (one presumed this would be an employee (or self-employed employee) rather than a customer).
7. This person would give one one's order.
8. Frank would then provide a map showing the route to the customer, which one would follow.
9. One would locate the customer and give them their order.
10. One would then return to Step 3.

And that, apparently, would be that. Easy.

This brief apprenticeship complete, all I had to do was wait for my kit to arrive. Lo and behold, the next day I received a large parcel containing kit to the worth of £80 (kindly provided for free): the ubiquitous bag, three branded T-shirts, a branded coat, a branded helmet, and a phone holder. I was also given a number: 496451. I had become a mere cog in the Deliveroo machine, a number rather than a named individual. Interestingly, though, customers would be told my name rather than my number – an insight into how the company portrays its riders to society in a different way to how it sees them itself. That, however, is a story for later.

As of now, only one thing mattered: according to Deliveroo, I was ready to ride. It was time to hit the road.

Chapter One: The First Ride

There is nothing impossible to him that will try.

Alexander the Great

Saturday, 23rd January 2021. The day on which I, as self-employed, had chosen to start my new (non) employment. Gusts of wind were beating the driving rain against the windows as I picked up my shiny new Deliveroo bag. I hesitated. I knew that to venture outside would certainly get me soaked to the skin and chilled to the bone while, being self-employed, I was of course under no obligation to do anything. On the other hand, I would earn some welcome money, and I don't like leaving a task unfinished. And I was bored. I was desperate to get outside and actually doing something.

There was no way of evading the inevitable. I put on my coat, picked up my gloves, and ventured outside to the garage to get my bike. My glasses were almost immediately plastered in raindrops as the chilly breeze bit into my face. I shivered, regretting my life choices even more strongly.

The inclement weather made me decide that, while I was happy to sacrifice my comfort in exchange for money (an interesting point for self-reflection), there was no need to expose myself unnecessarily to the elements. With this in mind I opened the Rider app and went online but remained sheltered in the garage for a few nervous minutes. It did not take long for an order to pop through. I examined the screen carefully. I did not want to exacerbate the situation in which, a vocal part of my subconscious was saying, I had very foolishly put myself.

I was very glad that I took this precaution as, although I do not want to appear prejudiced, when I learned that I would find my potential customer in a flat in Brixton I was not too keen to accept the order. I had heard a lot about that London district – very little of it positive. Deciding that accepting this order in the circumstances would be equivalent to a non-swimmer plunging into an Olympic diving pool, I rejected the order (the only time I ever did that) – and if my later experiences in Brixton are indicative of how this one would have gone, I am very relieved that I did.

After a few more minutes another order came through. This looked much more promising – to one Liz Atkinson, at 6, Kingsborough Mansions, over near Kennington, an area I knew reasonably well. I accepted the order, got on my bike, and headed off to collect it.

When I arrived at the restaurant the queue outside was stretching a good hundred yards down the road (restaurants being open for click-and-collect orders only). As a true Englishman I automatically went to join the end of the queue. However, I quickly realised that if I had to wait for my turn then I would be unlikely to find a happy customer when I arrived. After a brief struggle with my values, I marched to the front of the line and in through the door. I found my order sitting on the counter ready and waiting to go, but I made sure I showed my number to a member of staff in accordance with my instructions before loading the package into my bag and heading back to my bike. All well and good so far.

The cycle ride was easy enough – I knew the way for the most part and as by and large I enjoy cycling in any conditions, I started to feel a bit happier about my new job. Admittedly my hands, from which I had had to remove my gloves to lock up and unlock my bike, were already going numb, but otherwise I had no cause for complaint. I was soon standing outside Liz's address: a rather grand Victorian building which had obviously been converted into apartments. It seemed the job really was as easy as it sounded.

Possibly not. This was when things started to go slightly wrong. Liz had left a delivery instruction to ring her when I arrived so, having arrived, I did as such. Unfortunately, the building was right beside a major road and the noise of the traffic was exceptionally loud. I saw that the phone call had been answered but I could not hear a thing from the other end of the line. I could do little else but allow a couple of seconds to pass before announcing who I was, on the assumption that she would have started by asking who was calling. Having done that, I heard a vague murmuring noise but could not distinguish any words – she could have been telling me where to go or quoting Lenin for all I could hear.

'I'm very sorry, but the traffic is so loud that I can't hear what you are saying,' I shouted down the phone, barely able to hear myself speak as an ambulance howled past with siren blaring. Then there was a momentary lull as the cars which had pulled over to allow the ambulance past began to move off slowly but even as I asked her to repeat what she had said, the thunderous approach of a lorry drowned her reply in noise as well as me in spray. I took the initiative, hoping that she would at least be able to hear what I was saying even if I couldn't hear her.

'Seeing as I can't hear you,' I bellowed, 'can I suggest that you just come down and get the order from me?' I just about discerned an affirmative answer and breathed a sigh of relief. A minute or two later, a woman in her late twenties opened the front door. I was slightly unsure about the procedure now: Deliveroo had said to place the package on the ground before stepping back to facilitate social distancing, but the ground in question consisted of a large puddle. I considered that no customer in her right mind would be over the moon to see me placing her lunch in a puddle, so, in my position as self-employed and under no obligation to anyone, I made the executive decision to disregard such nonsensical rules. Better Covid than cholera from muddy puddles. I passed her the package.

And that was the end of the delivery. I cycled away feeling that it was something of an anti-climax. No fanfare of trumpets. No 'congratulations on completing your first delivery' message from my (non) employer. Not even a tip. Just a vague sense of relief that I had managed to get from A to B without any major difficulty.

I made my way slowly down the road before stopping to attempt to restore some life to my numb, wet fingers, while I waited to be (hopefully) assigned to another order. I'd only done one, but I had the feeling that completing deliveries was very addictive, and I had no intention of stopping before I absolutely had to.

I didn't have to wait long. I'd barely had time to register that my phone's battery was not taking kindly to its exposure to the elements on the handlebars of my bike, let alone warm my freezing fingers, when I was instructed to take a Burger King to Mr K. Richards, Montpelier House, Harperley Road. *This sounds posh,* I thought. The delivery instructions directed me to 'the red house at the end of the road.' As I collected the order and headed towards Mr Richards, I was picturing a large, detached house standing in its own grounds, with a flight of steps sweeping up to the front door.

Given that in London the area can change from dingily poor to luxuriously wealthy in a matter of yards, I was not immediately worried that my surroundings were somewhat grimy. I imagined that I would turn a corner and see in front of me Montpelier House dominating its surroundings, ornately barred gates revealing the Bentley on the drive... However, these optimistic ideas received short shrift when I turned onto Harperley Road. It ran parallel to a railway embankment, which largely prevented what natural light there was from brightening the scene, while dug into the embankment were several shady-looking car repair shops. The workers of said establishments were congregated outside smoking non-conventional cigarettes, as it were. I began to wonder where I would end up.

Then I saw something red at the end of the road. This matched the delivery instructions – up to a point. As I approached the building, I considered that 'house' was a somewhat generous description. Red it certainly was, but even 'shed' would have been charitable. 'Tumbledown shack' would have been more accurate. It was constructed of wood and seemed to be in a state of considerable disrepair. I noticed several holes in the walls. What was more, there did not seem to be a door to the place. I dismounted and stood looking around as the rain became noticeably heavier with a touch of sleet in the air.

Suddenly a man seemed to materialise from the side of the 'house'. He was thickset, with dark, greasy hair and untidy stubble. Bearing in mind that this was around 2.30pm in increasingly heavy rain, I was interested to see his choice of attire: barefoot, with a long dressing gown wrapped tightly around his extensive frame. He approached me.

'Is that for me?' Not the politest of greetings, but then again it was not out of keeping with the theme of the area.

'Er…' I considered my phraseology carefully. 'Is this Montpelier House?'

'Looks like it, doesn't it? Or weren't the instructions clear enough?' This was not said defensively, as if he was ashamed of his dwelling-place. It was demanded sarcastically, as a statement of the obvious.

I did not think it pertinent to give the reply which first came to mind. Instead, I smiled reassuringly. 'Yes, of course. I just wanted to make sure that I was giving the stuff to the right person.'

'Hurry up then, I ain't got all day.' He watched me intently as I fumbled with my bag. At last, my numb fingers allowed me to open the zip and retrieve his order. I handed it over as quickly as I could before saying goodbye and heading for a more salubrious area.

I was pedalling down the Wandsworth Road when the third order of the day popped up. There were two things that immediately seemed strange. Firstly, the restaurant had a name which was completely unfamiliar to me. Secondly, it was located at Units 11-12, Parkfield Industrial Estate. As a warehouse in an industrial estate is not a place I would normally choose to go out for a meal (on the hypothetical assumption that I had the funds to eat out), I had my suspicions about what I would find even as I accepted the order and set out. What I did find, however, was beyond anything I had considered possible.

Due to the fact that I had never been the way that the satnav was directing me before, I was concentrating on following the map rather than looking around me. I could see enough, though, to start doubting whether I was going to the right place. I came to a low, dark, narrow tunnel which took me underneath a railway line. Through the tunnel, turn left. Then through another tunnel. This one was damp as well as dark and filled with the echo of roaring engines as a couple of mopeds shot through going in the opposite direction. Then right. According to the sign, I was now in Parkfield Industrial Estate, charmingly located in a triangle of a few grimy acres bordered by three railways. This looked precisely nothing like somewhere you might find a restaurant. And it wasn't.

Welcome to Deliveroo Editions. Deliveroo-subsidised 'restaurants' that churn out cheap food on an industrial scale. Restaurants lacking the essential (according to the Oxford English Dictionary) element of restaurants – a place for customers to sit and consume their food on site. (Non) restaurants run by even more (non) employees of Deliveroo. (Non)sense.

11-12 Parkfield Industrial Estate was just the sort of warehouse one would expect to find enclosed by three railway lines in a dingy corner of Battersea. Metal. Grimy. Unpleasant. If it were not for the crowd of Deliveroo riders outside I would have concluded there and then that something was majorly wrong. But there they were: I was obviously on the right track. In the weeks to come, I would learn that this is one of the main characteristics of Editions places – the sheer number of riders at peak times must be seen to be believed. Imagine a beehive with swarms of bees coming and going. Then replace the hive with a warehouse, and the bees with Deliveroo riders, and you have some idea of what it is like. It is no exaggeration to say that at one moment you might have twenty or thirty mopeds parked up outside, with more coming and going the whole time. Leaving my bike locked up against a wall, I weaved my way through the crowd and pushed open the door.

I found myself in a square room with a flight of stairs ahead of me. There were several other riders crowded into the room, waiting. Bearing in mind that we were in lockdown, social distancing was somewhat lacking. Admittedly there were signs telling people to keep their distance and wear masks but neither of these rules were being enforced or obeyed.

To my left, in the far corner of the room, was a row of iPads on stands, with a sign telling me to sign in. First, I had to choose my employer – it's not only Deliveroo that uses these places, but Uber Eats and Just Eat as well. Then I put in my order number and was informed that it was currently 'in the oven'. A screen mounted higher up the wall had a list of all the order numbers with estimated times left before they were ready.

Up to this point I had not seen any of the place's workers. Suddenly, however, an exhausted-looking woman came hurrying down the stairs with an armful of order packages. She was instantly surrounded by a bevy of riders all pushing and shoving to get to the front. The air was full of noise.

‘Order 5634? You got 5634?’

‘I’m 2098!’

‘Is 7865 there?’

The woman forced her way through. ‘Hang on a moment! – wait please! Just a moment, please!’ She opened a door at the far side of the room and then reappeared behind a hatch which she opened in the wall. At least she was now protected from the crush, but there was no dissipation in the fight to get to the orders. I just stood on the edge of the melee, hoping that I would eventually get a chance to get to the front. The woman shoved a package through the hatch and shouted its number. A huge rider standing next to me recognised it as his and plunged towards the package like a boat launching into a stormy sea. A bow wave of other riders surged to each side as he ploughed through, grabbed his long-awaited cargo, and headed for the exit.

I was hoping that my number would come fairly near the end to allow the chaos to abate. On top of a slight concern that I might be suffocated or crushed to death, I was appalled at the situation. The nearest thing I could compare it to was feeding time at the zoo. It was as if the riders had abandoned any common feelings of courtesy in their frantic desire to get going.

Unfortunately for me, my number was the next one to come through the hatch. There was nothing for it: when in Rome… I entered the fray like a gladiator into the Colosseum.

'Yes – that's me – just coming through!' I proclaimed at the top of my voice, forcing my way to the front by using my bag as a battering ram against the wall of waiting men. I grabbed the package as the woman shoved it through the hatch. Now I had got to get out – and just at that moment the woman decided to speed up proceedings by introducing two more parcels to the game. Two riders came charging forwards – and I was right in their path. Borne along like a leaf before a tidal wave, I found myself back at the hatch. This was crazy. Force of circumstance, rather than any personal preference, dictated that I should stay put and wait for the crowd to thin. Eventually, I was able to beat a retreat and get back to my bike.

Now I had to get to the customer. This proved easy enough; the only incident worthy of note en route was when I noticed a boy walking a rabbit on a lead down the pavement: the first of many sights I would see in the course of my job which could only ever be found in London. I was soon standing outside a terraced house in Battersea – or at least a collection of flats cunningly disguised as a terraced house; to my eagle eye, however, the game was quickly given away by its four doorbells. Considering that the customer had left an instruction to call him when I arrived, the terrified voice which answered my call made me wonder if I hadn't misdialled someone with chronic neophobia.

'Y-y-yes? Wh-wh-who is it?' Anyone would think he was expecting an imminent attack. Maybe he was. I attempted to put him at his ease.

'Hi there, I've got your Deliveroo order just outside.' I was the image of reassuring politeness.

I heard a long-drawn-out sigh of relief. 'Ohhh, th-thank goodness. W-would you mind bringing it up?' The front door clicked unlocked. I pushed it open and entered, finding myself in a dark, narrow passageway ending in a flight of stairs. Climbing the staircase (not without difficulty with the huge bag on my back) I soon found myself outside the relevant door. I was about to knock when a quavering voice from within pre-empted me.

'J-j-just leave it outside the d-d-door, th-th-that will be fine.' The man was obviously petrified of something, but it wasn't for me to get involved. I unzipped my bag and placed his order on the doormat before making my exit. The three-point turn required in the confined space with my bulky kit created a fair amount of rustling and scraping; I could picture the poor man inside imagining an army of intruders preparing to burst in on him.

'OK, there you go. Have a nice day!' I called out as I headed back to the stairs. There was no reply. Perhaps he had fainted from shock.

Closing the front door behind me, I took a moment to consider my options. I had now been out for a couple of hours and was beginning to feel slightly concerned that (a) my core body temperature was at risk of dropping to a dangerous low and (b) my phone battery would not last for particularly long. To my warped priorities, the latter was a more serious worry – I had got cold before, but I had no idea what to do if my battery ran out mid-delivery. I wouldn't even be able to ring the customer to tell them that I couldn't find them but resorting to visiting every house in the relevant area would probably take about ten years. Despite these concerns, however, when another order came through, I just had to accept it.

It was an order from Pizza Hut: with four pizzas and two big bottles of fizzy drink, it was completely filling my bag. However, as it was downhill all the way I flew along like the express delivery rider I was. When I arrived, I was greeted by a very cheery man who enquired after my health like I was his long-lost son. After assuring him that I was very well, and learning that he was also in good health, I started to hand over his order. I felt optimistic that this delivery, at least, would be free of unpleasant incidents.

Suddenly his expression changed. 'Wasn't there something else?'

Castles in Spain came tumbling down. This was like my worst nightmare. Everything had seemed perfect, but obviously not – and then, to cap it all, he added that the missing item was the one he was looking forward to the most.

'Oh d-dear,' I began. It was probably the nervousness of starting a new job that deprived me of my speech: I rarely find myself at a loss for words. At the time, though, I was still a bit wet behind the ears (figuratively, as well as literally due to the rain). Or maybe my previous customer's stammer had been catching.

'The million pounds that I ordered?' As the grin spread across his face, I realised that this was probably his standard joke with delivery riders. This knowledge restored my natural verbosity.

'Oh yes!' I exclaimed. 'I should have said earlier – that item was out of stock and there was no suitable replacement. They sent their apologies and said that they would send it down by special delivery as soon as it arrives.'

'I'll look forward to that then,' he chuckled. 'Have a good day.'

If only such a happy conclusion could have boosted my phone battery as much as it boosted my spirits. Both had been almost on the verge of collapse but, while my spirits were now at a higher level than they had been for some time, the same could not be said for my phone battery. It was almost gone.

Falling in action on my first day (or indeed any other day) was not a particularly appealing prospect. My only solution, I decided regretfully, was to call it a day. Going offline, I closed the Rider app and headed homewards. Two and a half hours after I had set out, I put away my bike and exchanged the energy-sapping, icy rain of the London streets for the refreshing warm waters of my shower.

The last few hours had been formative. On the one hand, I had got out of the house (solving the boredom); met some interesting people (solving the loneliness); and I had earned £19.27 (starting to solve the finances). On the other hand, the job had already started to chip away at my humanity. The first indication of this had been my realisation that I was willing to forego my personal comfort for money; then five minutes later I had been queue-jumping against all my instincts – and despite realising this, I was willing to continue. With hindsight, this seems like the first step towards a vicious sub-circle of moral decline. At the time, and in the circumstances, I reckoned that any such concerns were more than countered by the £19.27. The only thing that could stop me was my phone's battery.

Overall, I was content with my first day as a Deliveroo rider. If I could keep this up, I was sorted.

Chapter Two: Getting Settled

Time and money are largely interchangeable terms.

Winston Churchill

The next important thing to do was to work out how to fit in my new job around my studies. It didn't take long for me to decide to go out for an hour or two at lunch time every day: this would break up the boredom of a long day studying as well as giving me a welcome breath of fresh(ish) air. I also did not particularly fancy riding around unknown parts of London's nastier areas in the dark.

On the flip side, riding at lunchtime would mean that I would have to forego my own lunch and find a different time to eat (if at all) – but I wasn't going to let a little thing like that get in the way of my new job. Another chip into my humanity: first prioritising money over comfort; now money over food. What would it prioritise over next?

Having made that decision, I was ready and raring to go. My next opportunity came a couple of days later in a break between tutorials when I found myself twiddling my thumbs again. Now, however, I knew exactly what to do: I headed out for another go at Deliverooing. It didn't take long to be assigned an order and soon I was cycling towards a fish and chip shop to collect the package.

It was on my way there that I came across another of London's stranger sights. Considering that it was raining steadily, I was slightly surprised when I noticed what seemed to be a very local patch of mist across the road. Or perhaps it was smoke? As I approached, I saw that it was by a church with a hearse pulled up outside. Then I noticed the red, green, and yellow flowers, the dreadlocks of the mourners… It was a Rastafarian funeral – and it dawned on me that the 'fog' was made of the fumes of the 'holy herb' that they were all smoking. I was somewhat concerned that I would get high from the quantity of 'wisdom weed' in the air (according to healthline.com, this is possible). I didn't notice any ill-effects though as I collected the order and cycled towards the customer.

En route to the customer, I always liked to try to picture what they would look like. Given that this naturally involved a fair bit of stereotyping, as all I had was their name and address, it's probably unsurprising that I experienced a range of (in)accurate results throughout my time riding. On this occasion, however, I never found out whether my prediction of Eleanor Baines was at all accurate. I arrived at her house but, before I could ring the bell, I was pulled up short by a notice on the door.

DELIVEROO RIDERS!

As this clearly pertained to me, I read on:

SOMEONE LIVING IN THIS HOUSE IS **EXTREMELY VULNERABLE** TO COVID-19. **DO NOT TOUCH** THE DOOR. **LEAVE THE PACKAGE ON THE DOORSTEP** AND WE WILL PICK IT UP ONCE YOU HAVE GONE.

Now while I can sympathise with people who are vulnerable to Covid, there are ways and means of carrying on. A bit of politeness would have been a start – 'please' and 'thank you' for instance. A lot of thought and effort had obviously been put into the notice: it was not a hastily scribbled post-it note but properly printed out and mounted on the door.

Probably more importantly from Eleanor Baines' perspective, while it might have seemed sensible to get her food delivered in order to avoid exposing herself to the virus outside, I didn't think that Deliveroo was really the safest option. For a start, few of the people involved in the order's preparation would have had time to wash their hands very often. This meant that before I turned up at her door the food would have been prepared by one set of grubby hands, packaged by another, and put into my oily, grimy hands by yet another. As for not touching the door, I found it unlikely that I would put any germs there which had not already found their way onto the package.

All in all, it would have probably been far safer to get a supermarket delivery where they enforced hygiene precautions. That might have meant having to make one's own meal though. I sensed that Eleanor Baines was the sort of person whose main priority was her own ultimate convenience rather than an excessive concern about hygiene.

Anyway, I did what I was told and headed off. I just hoped that I hadn't left too many smeary fingerprints on the package.

Curiously, I often found that I would get a couple of similar deliveries one day and then never get one like them again. It must have just been coincidence as the assignation of orders was solely (or at least, so I understood) based on the position of riders relative to the restaurant. Today was a case in point: on arrival at my next customer's door I was greeted by another sign but, after this, I was never to see one again.

Before I reached the second sign of the day, though, I faced an interesting episode at the restaurant. Minutes after leaving Eleanor Baines' door, I was assigned to pick up an order from a kebab shop about a mile away. The constant rain showed no evidence of abating as I accepted the order and set off, but I was already so wet that a bit more exposure to the elements was hardly going to make much of a difference.

As I approached the kebab shop I could see that, although it looked out onto the road I was on, the entrance was on a side-road while the building backed onto another parallel side-road a few yards along. With no particular interest, I noticed a police car pulling to a halt outside. Two policemen got out and, after a brief conversation, wandered casually round the corner to the entrance. Not really giving the matter much thought as I locked up my bike, I decided that they were just stopping for lunch.

They had hardly turned the corner when one of the shop's windows was pushed open and a man in an apron leaned out, glanced around furtively to see where the officers had gone, then withdrew inside and pulled the window shut. From my position outside, I could see him hurrying across to the back of the shop behind the counter and disappearing just as the policemen entered the front door.

Reckoning that something interesting was going on and that I would see more if I stayed where I was, I loitered by my bike. Through the window I observed the officers standing at the counter, apparently waiting to be served. Suddenly I heard a door open at the back of the building. Two men appeared carrying boxes which they shoved into the back of a small white van parked in the street, before climbing into the front.

Glancing for a moment into the restaurant, I noticed the man I'd seen earlier appearing behind the counter. From his gestures it looked like he was apologising for keeping the policemen waiting. Then, with a beaming smile and an expansive sweep of his arm, he placed a menu before them. There was nothing particularly unusual about this save for the fact that, just as he had the officers' attention, the van emerged from the side-street, slipped into the traffic, and headed away.

I decided that I'd seen all that was going to happen outside. I checked my order number then entered the kebab shop. As I came in, the warm smell of spicy meat provided a welcome change from the soaking, polluted air outside. The man behind the counter greeted me cheerfully, telling me that he would just finish the policemen's orders before getting mine ready.

Not being in any hurry, I was happy to wait. I unshouldered my bag and leant against the wall on the far side of the room to the officers, glad of the chance to shelter from the rain and warm up. Notwithstanding, I was in a bit of a quandary: should I tell the officers what I'd seen outside? They didn't seem to have any suspicion that anything out of the ordinary might have happened and now I was beginning to doubt it too: there was no reason why anyone should flee when the police had clearly come as mere customers rather than part of a raid. On the other hand, the men's behaviour had been peculiar to say the least.

Discretion took the better part of valour as the man behind the counter picked up a colossal kebab knife and started stripping meat off the slowly rotating lump of beef. I wasn't going to risk reporting him for a suspected crime when he was brandishing a two-foot blade just the other side of the counter, whether or not there were police present too.

Then one of the policemen's radios crackled into life. I could hear exactly what was said and, although his back was turned, from his demeanour it seemed that the man behind the counter could too.

‘A minor accident’s been reported roughly 300 metres from your location, involving a white van licence plate XX12 ABC and an unidentified car. Could you head down there to get some more details?’

At the mention of the van’s number plate the man behind the counter seemed to momentarily freeze. I hadn’t specifically noted the plate on the van I’d seen but it sounded vaguely familiar. The officers straightened up.

‘Can you keep the food warm for us? Hopefully this won’t take long but we’d better get down there,’ one of them said.

‘You’re sure you don’t want to wait?’ the man asked persuasively. ‘Just 30 seconds? Very nearly done…’ I might have been wronging him but he sounded rather keen to delay the policemen’s departure. Perhaps he wanted to give his associates down at the scene of the accident as much time as possible before the police arrived.

‘No, sorry, we’ve got to go,’ they broke in. ‘See you in a bit.’ With that, they made their way out of the door and jumped into their car. Its lights began to flash and it moved swiftly out into the traffic.

‘I shouldn’t think they will be long,’ I observed blandly. ‘What with it just being a minor incident.’

The man's friendly mood had vanished. 'You never know with these things,' he said curtly. 'Anyway, I'll get your order ready now.' The shop's atmosphere seemed tense as I waited, as if under the shadow of an imminent storm. Therefore, I was relieved when my order was complete although it meant heading back outside into the cold rain: an unpleasant but less oppressive atmosphere. Unfortunately, my route led the opposite way to the direction in which the police had gone and I didn't think I could justify taking a diversion to see what, if anything, was happening. Maybe I would find the time later…

With this thought in mind, shortly afterwards I turned up at the customer's address to find it located in a sort of compound. There was a high wall all the way around it with an automatic gate barring the entrance. Following the delivery instructions carefully, I dialled a code into the intercom and, after confirming who I was, the gate slid smoothly to the side. I had barely had time to get through when the gate glided back with a soft purr and locked firmly shut behind me. Unknown to me, I was now a prisoner. I would be unable to leave without the customer's express permission.

Despite the premises appearing to be impregnable, I looked for somewhere to lock up my bike – I have never liked taking chances in London. Having fastened it securely to a lamppost, I then examined my surroundings more closely. I was in what seemed to be an oasis of calm. Within the walls, which I now observed were topped with anti-intruder spikes, were six buildings arranged in a half-circle around a central car parking area. What struck me, though, was the silence. I don't know how but despite its proximity to a busy road the roar of traffic had vanished. It was a strange feeling, one which intensified when I found that, despite the security measures I had already seen, I had to dial the customer again on a different intercom system to get into their building. As I did, I spotted a CCTV camera above the door. It only required a moat to complete this impenetrable fortress – and, given the intensity of the rain, this didn't seem far from forming. I wondered what sort of people lived here, tucked away safely from any possibility of intruders. There must have been a few households to fill the buildings – each of which was probably divided into four or more apartments. What scared them? Or what did they have to hide?

As it happened, I never found out. I reached the customer's apartment door to find a sign which read as follows:

Dear Deliveroo Riders,

Thank you so much for bringing us our delivery. Much as we would like to be able to talk to you wonderful people face to face, unfortunately a member of our family is highly vulnerable and as such we regretfully have to ask you just to leave the delivery on the doorstep.

Have a lovely rest of the day!

This interested me. I noticed that it didn't specify the nature of the person's vulnerability. Maybe they were trying to hint that they were vulnerable to Covid when in fact they were at risk from something else: perhaps they were on the run from a rival gang? Or were they a retired spy worried about avenging assassins? The wording seemed almost excessively polite – was this the velvet glove that would expose an iron fist if I didn't leave fast enough?

Anyway, I wasn't going to hang around all day wondering about who was inside the apartment. I obediently deposited the order on the doorstep, headed back outside, unlocked my bike, and made my way to the gate. Normally, in a place like this, there will be a 'Press to Exit' button somewhere which lets one out, on the assumption that if someone has managed to get in they must be an authorised visitor and if not, it's better to have them out than in. Not here. I searched everywhere for a button (sometimes they aren't particularly obvious) but could find neither hide nor hair of one. I was trapped. Imprisoned within an unassailable citadel for the foreseeable future. To cap it all, I had handed over the food: I didn't even have any provisions with which to hold out.

I had noticed another intercom system but had initially thought that it was for the building immediately by the gate. Eventually, however, in desperation, I dialled the customer's number again. Thankfully I could remember it – once one has completed a delivery, one loses all the customer's details. I was slightly concerned about doing this: if I should have been able to get out independently, they might think I was hanging around for some nefarious purpose. What with all their other precautions, they might well have some method of disposing of unwanted guests. I was therefore relieved as they seemed to be expecting it and let me out without a quibble.

What really interests me is why that precaution was there. I have never encountered a system elsewhere whereby it was impossible to leave without permission. When added to all the other circumstances, it creates a whole realm of possibilities. It suggests that the inhabitants want the capability to detain someone – perhaps until the police arrived. That would imply that they are a sort of official secret: some of those people who live in a 'secure, undisclosed location'.

Probably there is some innocent explanation for it all: the unclimbable walls, the CCTV, the need to repeatedly gain permission to enter or exit, the capability to stop people leaving – but I like to think that I delivered to a retired spy.

My final delivery of the day was from Five Guys. As I pedalled towards the restaurant the traffic crawled to a halt. Overtaking the queue, I came to some blue flashing lights and saw that they surrounded an accident of some sort. Realising that I had come almost in a full circle since leaving the kebab shop earlier, with quickening interest I noticed the familiar shape of the white van: it had to be the accident to which the police had been called from the kebab-shop.

Upon arrival at the scene I grinned as I recognised the two policemen themselves. They obviously hadn't yet made it back to pick up their orders. Far more intriguing, however, was the fact that the van was being systematically stripped by a team of men in full protective gear. It looked like a drug squad. While this explained what I'd seen at the kebab shop to a degree, I could only think that the men involved had panicked at the arrival of the police – their flight must have been provoked by guilty consciences rather than any action of the police. Much as I would have liked to stay and watch the investigation further, I had a job to do. Regretfully, I pressed on towards Five Guys.

The customer turned out to be situated in a gleaming, brand-new apartment block near the US Embassy in Nine Elms. The rain had been getting increasingly heavy and by the time I arrived it was absolutely bucketing it down. I was drenched. Because of the weather I was wearing waterproof trousers, a raincoat, and my oldest pair of trainers – some rather dilapidated Nike Airs, one of which made a distinctive slapping noise as I walked due to the sole coming off at the heel, while the other trainer's air pocket had been punctured and so emitted a loud squeak (enhanced by the wet) with every step.

Thus, when I came through the revolving door into the foyer of this exclusive building, the water streamed off my coat and trousers and left an obvious trail behind me. Sounding like a sealion systematically eradicating a plague of mice, I *slapped* and *squeaked* towards the reception desk where the concierge was deep in conversation with two bowler-hatted gentlemen. As I approached all eyes turned to observe what had either blown in off the street or – what might have seemed more likely considering my appearance – been washed ashore from the nearby Thames. To their credit, none of them batted an eyelid at the bedraggled being which stood before them looking as out of place as a penguin in Trafalgar Square.

‘Good afternoon, how can I help you?’ The concierge was the very definition of politeness.

‘I have an order for number 3-014 – is this the right place?’

He picked up one of the phones on his desk and dialled a number. ‘Concierge speaking. Are you expecting a food delivery? … Excellent. I’ll send him up.’ He put the phone down. ‘It certainly is the right place, sir. Use lift five. The fourteenth room on the third floor.’ After ensuring that I had found the right lift, he turned back to his conversation.

A monstrosity gaped back at me from the lift mirror as I rode upwards. My eyes gleamed out of a face red with cold and exertion, smeared with chain oil from where I had rubbed my forehead with an oily glove. I was crowned with a wild crest of damp hair which shot up in all directions after its recent release from confinement in my helmet. Rivulets of water ran down my face and neck, washing the oil with it to give me a faint resemblance to a zebra. I stood in a puddle formed from the water which continued to drip from my sodden garments. I grinned as I wondered what on earth the concierge had thought. He had certainly concealed his opinions, but he could hardly have been delighted to see the mess that I was making in his nice foyer.

A conspicuous trail of water was still marking my route as I left the lift and walked down the plush corridor. The squeaking was painfully loud in the hushed atmosphere. Reaching my destination, I banged on the door then stepped back and waited for the customer to open it. The door swung open to reveal a man in his late thirties, dressed in pyjama trousers and a woollen jumper. He started at the sight of the apparition before him, then looked down his nose at me as he waited for me to open my bag. He clearly wanted as little as possible to do with such a frightful looking being. I decided to alter his impression of me slightly.

'Hello, there!' I beamed in my poshest possible voice. 'Got your old order here, eh, what?'

If anything, he jumped even more at this. Such an accent coming from a Deliveroo rider, particularly one looking like I did, really seemed to put him outside his comfort zone. Poor chap, having to cope with such an apparition in his expensive residence. He seemed to forget that if he hadn't put in the order in the first place then I wouldn't have got into such a state, let alone into the building.

'Th-thanks a lot,' he managed to say, before retreating quickly and closing the door. I headed back towards the lift, leaving him with a nice puddle outside his door to step in next time he went out. Calling a cheerful 'thank you' to the concierge as I passed back through the foyer, I logged out of the Rider app and set my face homewards.

When I got back, my soaking hands were too numb to unlock the garage door to put away my bike. I found myself standing for a good five minutes outside the door, alternately trying to beat the circulation back into my fingers and attempting to hold the key with one hand while using the other to try and push it round. When I finally got inside, though, the amazing feeling of a warm shower, dry clothes, and a mug of hot chocolate made it all worthwhile – to say nothing of the healthier bank balance. I had only been riding for a couple of days, but I was satisfied with my new job.

Those first two days riding had been ideal. Well, perhaps not ideal, but I'd seen some interesting things and only had one or two minor issues. Nothing serious. I was naïve enough to think that things would always be this easy.

Chapter Three: The Grim Reality

Misfortunes never come singly. It never rains but it pours.

English sayings

Wednesday morning dawned with an effort. The weather had dried up slightly but as I tried to study it seemed that the sun was about as motivated to break through the lowering clouds as I was to prepare for my next tutorial. By midday, I had had enough. I threw down my pen, grabbed my Deliveroo bag, and headed for the door. There was more than a hint of rain in the air and it felt like it was getting dark already; apparently the sun had given up its struggle as quickly as I had given up my studies for the day.

I began to feel more optimistic as I collected the first order that was assigned to me without incident. On the way to the customer the traffic was thick – or rather, stationary – but in the cycle lane I was able to move fast. There was another cyclist just ahead of me, moving at the same speed. Just a typical cycle ride through London.

Then everything changed in a moment. We were coming up behind a bus when suddenly its door opened and a passenger stepped down into the cycle lane without even checking – right into the path of the cyclist in front of me. There was a sickening thud as they collided – a scream from the ex-passenger – and the cyclist was soaring through the air, somersaulting, then rolling down the road as her bike, riderless, hit the curb and flipped over.

I skidded to a stop, quickly assessing the situation. There was a bit of blood from the groaning cyclist; meanwhile, although the passenger didn't seem to have suffered any major physical harm, her rapid gasps for breath showed her shock at the collision. The bus driver had already jumped down and was anxiously trying to help the cyclist up.

Humanity urged me, too, to offer some assistance. The practicality of someone's dinner going cold on my back told me to get moving. It was like a real-life conflict between hard-line capitalism and socialism: was my primary responsibility to the customer or to society? *I can't just let the customer starve*, I decided. My conscience was calmed by the fact that the bus driver and passenger were already assisting the cyclist. Discretely, I faded back into the traffic and continued my journey.

Soon I was outside the customer's address – a not particularly salubrious building in central Brixton. If the delivery instructions hadn't already told me that I was heading for a flat, I would have been able to deduce as much from the intercom keypad by the door. Not really thinking about what I was doing, I started pressing one of the numbers shown on my screen into the pad. Then I realised that I had entered the building's number rather than that of the flat.

Stupid, I told myself, looking for the usual 'cancel' button. There wasn't one. *Really?* It seemed strange – after all, everyone puts in the wrong code occasionally. Nevertheless, after a careful scrutiny of the pad, I was confident that there was no way of deleting the number which was now waiting for me to press the green 'call' button.

Press the green call button. There was an idea. Once the call had ended, I'd then be able to call the right number. Of course, that would involve calling a different, unsuspecting resident, but hopefully they wouldn't mind. There would be a bit of a problem if they turned out to be waiting for a different Deliveroo order, but I decided that I would cross that bridge if I came to it. I pressed the green button.

I quickly ran through my options as I waited for someone to answer. I could either explain my problem immediately or pretend that I thought that I was ringing the right person. The former, I reasoned, would both make me sound like a nitwit who couldn't cancel a simple call and probably irritate the resident into the bargain. The latter also might well irritate the resident but would save my face to some extent; furthermore, depending on what they said, there was the potential for some fun. As the resident was likely to be irritated whichever path I took, I opted for the fun one.

There was a click as someone answered my call. A pause. Then a deep, passive-aggressive voice came crackling over the intercom.

‘Errrm… Who is it?’

‘Hi, I’ve got your Deliveroo order here,’ I answered cheerfully.

‘Errrm… you’ve got my what?’ The disembodied voice floating out of the speaker took on a more puzzled tone.

‘Your Deliveroo order. Your KFC,’ I explained.

‘Errrm… I don’t think so.’ The voice now had the tone of a parent addressing an argumentative three-year-old. It did not encourage further conversation.

‘Oops, I must have dialled the wrong number. Sorry.’ The words had hardly left my mouth when there was another click as the owner of the voice ended the conversation.

I could now dial the right number, ensuring that I did so carefully. This time nobody spoke. The door clicked open, and moments later I was clumping up an unlit, narrow staircase towards the second floor. It was all dark inside. All I could hear was the occasional dripping of water from my damp clothes. Arriving at the top of the staircase, I peered into the gloomy passage. Two silent, dark figures loomed at the end of it. I stopped.

‘Yu ‘right, bruv?’ The voice was intimidating. I could just make out black puffer jackets, tracksuit bottoms, and a faint but unmistakable smell of marijuana. It felt like a stand-off between Wild West gunfighters as we stood facing each other from opposing ends of the dark passage – the perfect place for a crime to be committed. Armed only with a dinner, I felt at a distinct disadvantage – any amount of weaponry could have been tucked away inside those jackets.

'I've got a Deliveroo order for Asman Khan,' I announced.

'Do yu? Well, we ain't stopping yu.' They weren't doing anything to facilitate me either. A door opened, letting a beam of light into the passage, and a third figure, identically dressed, appeared. The first speaker addressed the newcomer. 'Yu din't tell us yu was getting Deliveroo, man.'

'Yeah, 's easier than going out. Y' know what happened las' time.'

Preferring not to wonder what had happened last time, I stepped forward, opening my bag. 'Asman?' He nodded and took the package. 'Have a nice day,' I smiled, realising that this sounded slightly out of place in the setting, and made my way back down towards the front door.

My relief at getting back outside into the fresh air was somewhat counterbalanced when I looked at the time and realised that I had an online tutorial very shortly. I would much rather have stayed out and done a few more deliveries, even considering what I'd seen, but I valued my education enough to force myself to head back to the uninspiring atmosphere of my bedroom.

There was nothing wrong with the content I was learning, but the online atmosphere was really getting to me.

I was about halfway home when I pulled up at some traffic lights at a roundabout, alongside the collection of other cyclists and motorcyclists that one inevitably finds at the front of queues in London. As also usually happens, several of the cyclists started going early so they were out ahead of the rest in the middle of the junction when the light turned green. Those of us obedient to the Highway Code now began to move.

The heavy revving of the motorbikes' engines as they raced forwards was instantly followed by a screech of brakes. One of the cyclists already ahead had started to change direction – right into the path of one of the motorbikes. It was too late. There was a smash as the motorbike ploughed into the cyclist. Both riders came off, sprawling across the road, while the motorbike span viciously in a circle. Pedestrians rushed into the road to help while the rest of the traffic came to a grinding halt. Ambulances were being called; the motorcyclist was sitting up but a group of people had knelt around the cyclist who was lying motionless in the road.

Being the socially useful citizen that I'd like to think I am, I decided that there was no reason for me to hang around. As my only real first-aid training had taken place in primary school about 12 years ago, there didn't seem to be anything that I could provide.

Concluding that it would be hypocritical to just stand there pretending to be useful I headed on home, quite shaken by the fact that I had seen two crashes in one day when I had never seen one before. It reinforced the message that anything can happen – and probably will just when one's not expecting it.

Little did I think that the next day would bring even more excitement.

Soon after starting riding I had become aware of a news story from another city which involved Deliveroo riders. It seemed that gangs in the city were stopping riders and forcing them at knifepoint to hand over the food in their bags. In response, some riders were starting to carry knives. Matters came to a head when a large group of youths surrounded two riders emerging from a restaurant; the riders pulled knives and fought their way through, during which action one teenager was killed and two more ended up in intensive care. Thankfully, I never experienced anything like that. Not quite, anyway.

Since I had come to live in London I had heard some local stories, not necessarily involving Deliveroo riders, about a crime hotspot in the vicinity of where I was riding. A spree of muggings had recently been compounded by a rather nasty murder. It being on the fringes of my Deliveroo patch, I hadn't yet visited the area. That state of affairs was about to change.

When I went out the next day at my usual time, I was rapidly assigned to an order. I got to the restaurant without incident and was provided with the route to the customer, realising in passing that it would take me right through the alleged danger zone. I wasn't worried. I had never seen a crime in progress before; after all, I reasoned, mugging was something that happened to other people on dark nights when I was safely tucked up in bed. This, on the other hand, was broad daylight with plenty of other people around. Admittedly, I was obviously carrying food and my phone was exposed on my handlebars, but things like that didn't happen to me. I clearly hadn't learned any lessons from the day before.

This is where I could use a bit of dramatic licence. I could portray the scene something like this: *As I came into the danger area, I noticed a Victorian hearse drawn by four magnificent black horses with majestic plumes on their heads weaving silently through the traffic. A sense of foreboding overwhelmed me. The air seemed to get suddenly colder as the wind picked up, whistling ominously as it swayed the bare branches on the trees. The bag on my back acted as a sail, catching the gust of wind as the buildings on either side funnelled it down the road. I was propelled forward, accelerating effortlessly and unwillingly towards my fate. A cold hand seemed to clutch at my heart – or maybe it was just the icy fingers of the wind.*

The reality, however, was nothing like that. The hearse was just another one of London's unexpected sights, and a bit of breeze in mid-winter was hardly unusual. I was simply and blithely wending my carefree way to the customer without a thought that anything out of the ordinary might happen.

The wind died away again as I began to approach a large junction, weaving slowly through the stationary vehicles between the outer and middle lane. I was manoeuvring around a bus when it happened. I came face to face with a man. A not particularly nice-looking man. Not to say an unusual place to come across a pedestrian. Our eyes met for a second. A grim smile spread across his face. His hand flashed to his pocket. There was a glint of metal as a knife blossomed in his hand. And he came charging down the length of the bus towards me.

Adrenalin coursed through my veins. To turn around would take too long. The only way to go was forward. Straight into the arms of a knife-wielding maniac.

I slammed my foot down onto my pedal and accelerated hard. Time seemed to stand still as I shot towards my assailant. He faltered for a moment as my unexpected manoeuvre caught him off guard – giving me the chance to knock the knife to one side with one hand a split second before I shoulder-barged him full in the chest. He staggered back against the side of the bus, while the knife clattered onto the tarmac. As I barged past, the image of a horrified passenger behind the bus window was imprinted on my mind like a photograph.

Then I was racing through the traffic lights and across the junction with a wildly beating heart as the impact of the last ten seconds caught up with me.

I slowed down to give myself a chance to recover. I didn't want to turn up at the customer's house looking like a nervous wreck. Thankfully, by the time I reached the address, my heart had slowed to its normal rate and I was breathing more easily.

I pressed the relevant buzzer by the front door. Without having to speak to anyone over the intercom, the door clicked unlocked. Pushing it open, I stepped inside. The door slammed shut behind me and cut off at a stroke the roar of the traffic outside. All was silent. Finding myself in a narrow stairwell, I began making my way up. Rather unhelpfully there was no indication of which floor the customer's flat was on but, as he was Number 4, I guessed that he would be on the first floor. I was about to push the door open to access those rooms when a deep voice boomed out from above, echoing around the narrow stairwell. The way it was said made it sound as if every word started with a capital letter.

'You Have Another Floor to Go!'

My heart leapt almost into my mouth. I had had no idea that there was anyone there – the staircase had been as silent as the grave. It was a creepy thought that a man had been watching me without my knowledge, and still more that he had anticipated my movements. At least

I didn't need to go on a wild-goose chase into a random part of the building.

After satisfying myself that my heart had returned to its proper place, I headed on up the stairs until I came face to face with the customer. He was watching me silently from the landing: a man in his thirties, wearing blue jeans and a sweater. Cold green eyes stared out of a completely expressionless face. He said nothing. He seemed to be looking right through me. Not for the first time that day, a shiver ran down my spine.

'James?' I asked. He nodded without a sound. I opened my bag and he reached out a hand in anticipation. As I passed over the bag, his fingers seemed to mechanically open and close around the handle like a robot. He withdrew his hand but continued to stare at me unblinkingly. I felt like a juicy centipede being watched by a lizard.

I tried to smile. 'Have a nice day.' There was no response. He could have been made of stone for all the reaction he gave. I headed down the stairs, feeling those icy, reptilian eyes boring into my back the whole way down. As I pulled the door shut behind me, I breathed a deep sigh of relief.

Enough was enough. Emotionally exhausted, I unlocked my bike and headed home. The state I was in, I fully expected some new danger to be lurking behind every corner to finish me off properly. I could hardly believe it when I pulled up at my front gate ten minutes later without incident.

I don't think that I have ever been more thankful to get home safely. For the first time, I began to wonder whether I should continue riding: in two days I had had more near misses than I would have thought possible in a year. To carry on would inevitably increase the risk of being stabbed, run over, or knocked off my bike. That, though, would take me right back to square one regarding boredom and finances – my university situation seemed unlikely to change any time soon.

I decided to keep riding – money was now officially prioritised over safety, as well as comfort and food.

At least I now knew what I could expect. Stabbings, muggings, and reptilian customers hadn't featured in the glowing job description on Deliveroo's website but now I had a more realistic picture of what might happen. As the Scouts say, *Be Prepared.* I could prepare for the worst now that my nonchalant assumptions of continued safety had been blown out of the window.

In the back of my mind, though, the peaceful fields of Oxfordshire seemed increasingly preferable to London's action-packed streets.

No, I told myself firmly. *You can't let yourself be beaten.* I gritted my teeth and settled down for the long haul.

Chapter Four: More Revelations

Slavery is a weed that grows on every soil.

Edmund Burke

The weather can have a unique capacity for setting the tone of a day. At least, that's how it often seems. When the sun is shining from a cloudless blue sky and the birds are singing in the trees, the tips flow freely and the traffic moves easily. One feels relaxed and content; all one's worries fade as the gentle breeze blows the cobwebs from one's mind. However, when the rain starts to fall from leaden skies and an icy gale begins to suck the heat from one's body, the birds hunch up inside their feathers, the customers get rude, the traffic piles up – and one ends up at some dodgy places.

It was raining heavily the next Tuesday when I was instructed to pick up an order from Units 13-15 Battersea Heliport Industrial Estate. I'd never been there before but there were no prizes for guessing that this would be another Editions set-up. I arrived, soaked to the skin, to find the appropriate part of the said estate to be a short cul-de-sac with single-storey warehouses on either side of the road. Most of them seemed to be car repair workshops: the smell of oil and rubber was strong, accompanied by the sound of metal clashing against metal. Not for the first time I doubted whether I was at the right place. Again, not for the first time, it was the swarm (for want of a more appropriate collective noun) of Deliveroo riders outside one of the buildings that showed me I was right.

I locked up my bike and headed over to the door. A stream of other riders was going in and out of the smallish, solid-looking, metal building. All seemed well and good so I copied their example. The door creaked on its rusting hinges as I hauled it open and stepped inside.

The heavy door clashed shut behind me as I found myself in an incredibly confined space. The heat hit me like a punch in the face. As I moved forward the bag on my back prevented me from turning to either side in the short, low-roofed passage which opened out onto a scene direct from the sweatshops of south-east Asia. On either side of the central walkway were four or five kitchen bays, each containing three or four 'chefs' working at top speed. They were mostly men in their late thirties or forties – older than the riders – and were all clearly immigrants. Sweat glistened on their exhausted, tightly drawn, red faces. Some were pulling trays in and out of ovens, others were running backwards and forwards with ingredients; some were frantically mixing things in bowls, others were shoving food into bags. The air was unbearably hot and sticky, and it was deafeningly loud: shouts for ingredients, rattling saucepans, banging oven doors. I felt like I had entered a new, nightmare existence.

Then I noticed the person who was obviously in charge and I could not believe what I was seeing. A very attractive young woman was directing operations in a highly efficient manner while the men did what she told them unquestioningly. She noticed me and several other riders who had followed me in and came over to us.

'Hi, what order numbers have you got?' The voice was almost cultured. We each told her our number and she dashed off, returning moments later with one of the orders and informing the rest of us that ours would be ready shortly. At least my departure should be sooner rather than later, but immediately would have been ideal. My only option was to stay inside and wait.

The seconds seemed to crawl past as my eardrums were pounded and I struggled to breathe in the suffocating atmosphere. I felt like I was in a sauna as sweat poured from me. I took my glasses off as they had completely steamed up but was quickly forced to replace them as their slippery plastic frames seemed intent to slide through my clammy fingers. The nightmarish quality of the setting increased dramatically as I peered through the misty glass at wraith-like figures that whisked back and forth, the sound of their passing unnoticeable against the intensity of the overall noise.

My relief was therefore great when in a few minutes the manager returned and handed each of us the right order. I was exceedingly impressed: she had managed to remember four 4-digit numbers and to whom each one belonged. Even in the chaotic atmosphere, I found time to wonder what such an obviously highly intelligent person was doing working in a place like this.

Finally, I could leave. I turned around, made my way back down the passage, and pulled open the door. London's polluted atmosphere had never tasted so good as the door clanged shut behind me. For a moment or two I just stood there in the cool, refreshing rain, enjoying the feeling that I had woken up from a particularly nasty dream but that sanity had now returned.

There wasn't time to worry about what I had seen for the moment, though. As I pedalled towards the customer, vague recollections from when I was signing up crossed my mind of Deliveroo's website containing glowing descriptions of how it was helping people set up their dream restaurants. This, it seemed, was how they were approaching the task.

A few minutes later I pulled up to some traffic lights at a crossroads. The road approaching from the left was bordered by a solid metal wall which surrounded a development site. On the road surface I could see a large pool of some sort of liquid with an oily tint. For some reason I had a sense of foreboding that something nasty was about to happen. Which it did.

An engine roared as a car, approaching from the left, accelerated to try and get across the junction while the light remained green. Then the light went red. The driver slammed on his brakes – the car skidded violently – slewed around – and smashed into the metal wall. Its bonnet crumpled amid a shower of sparks as metal grated on metal with a horrendous screech. And some of the sparks landed in the pool of liquid – which exploded into a sheet of flame.

I was horrified as the flames immediately engulfed the shattered front of the car. Dropping my bike, I ran towards the blaze as the driver scrambled out and dived to safety. The intense heat forced me to retreat, not that there was any need to get closer now that the driver was safe. The smell of burning rubber and oil filled the air, making me cough.

As I could hear other passers-by calling the fire brigade, I stood back and awaited the arrival of the professionals. They didn't take long. Within a minute or two I heard a siren and a fire engine screamed to a halt by the burning car. Firemen leapt out and in a matter of seconds the flames were blanketed in a deluge of foam. More sirens heralded the approach of an ambulance with a couple of police cars. I guessed that the police would close the road to enable the incident to be cleared up – but I needed to get through to complete my delivery. Reckoning that there were enough other witnesses to provide an accurate account if necessary, I remounted my bike and shot across the junction just as the policemen started getting out cones to block off the road.

I can't remember what the customer was like. My mind was still full of what I had just seen, both at the industrial estate and the junction. However, I wasn't shaken enough to want to go home yet. Better to forget about it on the job than to worry about it at home. The fact that if it hadn't been for the job, I wouldn't have seen what I had was irrelevant to my increasingly warped priorities. I was soon on my way to pick up a KFC.

The shop was crammed with riders waiting for their orders. We easily outnumbered the three or four KFC workers who were desperately working to reduce the backlog which had clearly built up. Every couple of minutes one of them would shout out a number and shove a packet onto the counter, but in that time yet another rider would have come in. It made my job feel easy, relaxed, and stress-free.

Eventually, my number was called. As I put the package in my bag I had a feeling that it looked a bit smaller than what I could see of the inventory. However, there was no way I was going to check with the woman who'd compiled it. She was already frantically collecting the next order and I had no desire to make her life even more difficult by being pernickety. In the circumstances a mistake wasn't unlikely, but I decided that the customer had no moral right to complain given the effort that was being expended on his behalf. He might be unaware of it but that was too bad.

In any event, I could see that he had left a delivery instruction to leave the package on his doorstep. I didn't even have to speak to him. If there was a problem then he would have to sort it out on his own. But *the best laid plans of mice and men...*

As I pedalled up the road to his house, I could see him waiting outside – an exceptionally tall, burly man with thinning hair. He clearly didn't trust the rider to follow his instructions, and his behaviour suggested that I wasn't the only one to suspect there was something wrong. I handed him the package but, instead of thanking me and letting me go on my way, he opened it up and inspected its contents. Grimly, he held up a single can of Pepsi. It was not, it seemed, what he was expecting.

'This doesn't look like two 2-litre bottles to me,' he said. Talk about stating the obvious.

'No, it doesn't,' I agreed. There didn't seem to be much else to say. I would have been happy to leave it there and get a move on, but his demeanour suggested that the conversation was not at an end. I could see the question hovering on the tip of his tongue.

'... aren't you going to go and replace it then?'

I had zero desire to cycle all the way back to KFC and get the bottles. Not only would it be a three-mile round trip, but I had no proof that I was in fact entitled to two 2-litre bottles of Pepsi. I knew that, even at the best of times, getting them out of the massively overworked and even more massively underpaid staff would be a good deal harder than extracting blood from a stone.

Considering their state when I had picked up the order, the difficulty would be multiplied ten-fold. Knowing that he was unlikely to accept those as sufficient reasons not to go back, I pre-empted him.

'I'm very sorry that you haven't got what you ordered,' I said, 'but my job is simply to take the food from the restaurant to you. I have nothing to do with the preparing of the order. If it's not all there then that's KFC's fault, so you'll have to raise it with them.'

This might have been true, but KFC was at the other end of a phone call and a mile and a half away whereas Muggins was standing right in front of him holding a conveniently sized bag. I could sympathise with his unconvinced expression particularly as, whoever was to blame, it certainly wasn't him. It was time to make my getaway before he started arguing.

'Well, I'm very sorry but I've got to get on so goodbye.' I backed away hastily, turned my bike round, and vanished out of his life into the London traffic. Like Alexander the Great cutting the Gordian knot, I had solved the problem in a way which suited me but which was hardly the way it should have been done. I had the distinct feeling that I was leaving the situation in an unsatisfactory state – but at least he had something. Moreover, I didn't need to go back to KFC, and the KFC workers' stress levels wouldn't have to cope with sorting out the problem (at least, until they got a phone call from the customer).

In other words, it could have been worse for everybody.

With such thoughts floating around my mind, I made my way home. It was an uneventful ride until I turned into my road when I saw three boys swaggering down the middle of the street towards me. They looked like they were hardly out of primary school but two things about them instantly caught my attention: they were dressed like miniature replicas of the men I'd met in Asman Khan's flat a few days previously; and one of them was carrying a firework in one hand and a lighter in the other.

I did not like the look of this. The boy with the firework was waving it around and pretending to light it while his companions were filming him and shouting encouragement. Even if they didn't light it intentionally, there seemed to be a good chance that it would be set off by accident – and with the cars and houses on both sides of the street, some expensive damage could be caused. I reckoned I should do something to prevent it.

The boys saw me coming and moved to block my passage. I smirked, thinking how easy it would be to barrel through them compared to the knife-wielding mugger I'd dealt with before. Doing that here, though, would probably incite a rocket through my bedroom window when they saw me pulling into my drive. I pulled to a halt.

‘Deliveroo, huh?’ the firework-wielding individual grunted aggressively in what was obviously an attempt to make his unbroken voice sound deeper. I nodded.

‘Who’s it for?’ demanded one of the others in an equally squeaky voice.

‘Whom,’ I corrected. This seemed to catch him off his guard. He looked at his companions and opened his mouth to speak but then shut it again.

‘What’s the customer’s name?’ piped up the third boy with a clever grin.

I decided not to tell them that my bag was empty. ‘Tell me yours and I’ll tell you if it’s for you,’ I countered.

Firework Boy stepped closer, clicking his lighter. I took my phone off its holder and pretended to flick through to a new page. ‘What did you say your name was?’

The boys clearly didn’t know what to make of me. One moment I was correcting their grammar and the next I was apparently prepared to believe they might be my customers. They stood slightly back, bunching together as if each was waiting for one of the others to make the next move.

Suddenly I lifted my phone and took a photo of the three of them. All their faces, as well as the firework, were clearly visible in the picture. I looked Firework Boy straight in the eyes. ‘Get moving,’ I ordered, ‘and if that firework causes any damage round here I'm going straight to the police with this photo.'

He glared back up at me. I stared at each of them in turn. One by one, their eyes dropped. Then they began to slink away. I stood and watched them go, waiting until they were out of sight before making my way to my front gate.

What on earth was wrong with this city, where twelve-year-olds were wandering around with fireworks and apparently already embarking on a career of crime?

Still, I had proved to myself that I wasn't completely socially irresponsible. If I hadn't stopped, I told myself, some significant damage could have been caused.

Chapter Five: Finding My Way

Rules are for the obedience of fools and the guidance of wise men.

Harry Day

I always used to take stories of people driving off cliffs and into rivers because their satnav told them to with a ladleful of salt. Not now. I used to think that, if I were in that sort of situation, I wouldn't go that far, but now I can see how it happens. Once you become dependent on it and are in an unfamiliar area, it can be hard to break away and choose a different route. Satnav certainly gave me a couple of unusual – to say the least – experiences while out riding for Deliveroo.

Later that same week, a delivery took me along the South Circular before heading off round into the back of Brixton to get to the customer. I reached them without any difficulty and handed over their order. Everything had gone without a hitch. Glancing at my watch, I was surprised at the time: apparently time flies when Deliverooing as well as when having fun (an alternative conclusion being, of course, that Deliverooing and having fun are synonymous).

Why the time had gone so fast was not my immediate concern, however. More pressing was the fact that I had a tutorial in 45 minutes and needed to be ready for it (I doubted anyone else in my class would be but, despite loathing online tutorials, I wanted to profit as much as I could from the teaching available).

Therefore, gratified with how easy the day had been, I closed the Rider app and opened City Mapper to find the quickest way home. This app was recommended to me as great for getting around London but I had not actually used it before – this was going to be a bit of an experiment. It found a route and off I went.

Knowing roughly where I was, I assumed that I would be taken straight across Brixton. I was. But I didn't have the least suspicion of which part of Brixton I would go through.

Within a few minutes I came to some traffic lights. I was on a minor road joining, or rather crossing, a major one. Across the road, on the street that City Mapper was instructing me to take, I could see a sign welcoming me to Brixton. I was not at all surprised by this, bearing in mind where I knew I was. The surprise came a moment later when the light turned green and I pedalled towards the sign which I now realised was actually welcoming me to HMP Brixton.

The prison entrance must be just off the street there, I deduced. As I was interested to see what it would be like, I slowed down and looked around me as I progressed along the street. Then I saw a barrier across the road with a guard post and a sign saying 'BRIXTON PRISON – STRICTLY NO UNAUTHORISED ACCESS'.

Maybe I should turn round. However, the satnav was telling me to go straight ahead, there was (inexplicably) no one in the guard post, and there was enough room to get my bike around the barrier. I didn't hesitate. Decisive action being my motto, I cycled straight into the prison premises. My mind was busy thinking of what to say should I be accosted: would a guard be able to tell the difference between a stereotypical Deliveroo rider who might not know any better, and a King's College law student who definitely should? Admittedly, my appearance at that moment would not have encouraged identification as the latter. I decided that if I were stopped, I would gesticulate wildly at the map – which was undoubtedly telling me to proceed straight ahead – and say very little. *Play the stereotype.* Doubting that I could do a convincingly foreign accent to enhance the stereotype further, I instead decided that I would just try and sound rather less posh than people tell me I normally do.

In the event, however, these plans were not needed. I passed various entrances – 'Family visitors', 'Other visitors' – while on both sides towering walls mounted with coils of barbed wire and shards of broken glass emphasised where I was. A few people were walking around but, while they gave me curious glances, they made no move to stop me. I have often found that if I act as if I have every right to be doing what I am (however outrageous), people leave me alone. The technique certainly worked here as I pedalled blandly along just as if I was cycling down Clapham High Street.

I could now see that the road terminated in a car park surrounded by the high prison wall. It seemed that I was coming to a dead end. I wondered what to do. It was hardly feasible to climb over the wall, but I didn't really fancy going back the way I had come. As I weighed up the options, City Mapper saved the day with an unusual instruction.

'Progress for 25 yards, then dismount and wheel your bike through the hole in the wall.'

I was astounded. Had City Mapper somehow found about an escape route from the prison? Would I join a stream of desperate prisoners participating in the Great Escape of the 21st Century? Did the authorities know about this 'hole in the wall'?

I certainly couldn't see anything that looked like a hole: the wall looked impregnable to me. Just then I noticed some builders' fencing bordering a bit of pavement. Dismounting in accordance with my directions, I pushed my bike up the curb before turning to discover that the path led, indeed, to an entrance in the wall. Without any exaggeration, with my Deliveroo bag on my back it was a tight fit to get through. Once I had squeezed through, however, I was relieved to find myself safely back on a public highway.

All that I could imagine is that the 'hole in the wall' was some kind of old entrance to the prison, but why it was accessible by any member of the public was beyond me. There were no signs on it – like there were at the main entrance – barring entrance. How City

Mapper knew about it, though, and saw fit to send me through it remains a mystery.

I should mention that I have since stopped using City Mapper. I did like some of its interesting features, such as its estimation of the calories one would have used and how much money one would have potentially saved by cycling rather than taking another means of transport. However, I came to believe that its method of calculating such estimates was somewhat flawed when it told me that, by cycling back from a location in Battersea, I had saved £76. I wondered whether it was basing its calculations on the assumption that I would otherwise be chartering the Royal Yacht or a private helicopter. This was not something to make me stop using the app though – as long as it got me home safely then I didn't mind what it told me afterwards. It was what it told me to do whilst getting home that started to become the problem, such as when it tried to get me to cycle over the Hammersmith Flyover – a dual carriageway which technically has a 30mph speed limit but which, in practice, people roar over at much greater speeds (when it is not clogged with traffic). Not wishing to end up at the bottom of a pile-up, I decided that what with taking me through a prison, another occasion when (again blindly following its directions) I had ended up in Islington (a good few miles from where I wanted to be) by accident, and now trying to get me killed, City Mapper could give way to Google Maps – which I have found completely satisfactory in every respect.

While on this subject, it was not only City Mapper which gave me trouble with navigation. A week or two after the prison adventure, the Deliveroo Rider app itself got me into a bit of a sticky fix. Although this app allows one to access either Google or Apple Maps through it to give better directions, I usually just made do with the Rider app – otherwise I had to have two apps open, both of which were using my location and thus burning my battery a lot faster. The slower my battery drained, the longer I could stay out and the more money I could earn. I was even prioritising money over ease of working.

Everything had flowed smoothly for the best part of a week when I logged into the app one sunny lunchtime, hoping that this happy state of affairs would continue. Within a few minutes I had got a stacked order from an unremarkable restaurant, had got to the first customer without incident and was on my way to the second one – Ahmed. I instantly suspected that there might be something wrong as I could see that his postcode was SW4 (Clapham), but the map was taking me right into Brixton. Optimistically, I told myself that the SW4 patch probably spread a bit farther than I had previously supposed. The app had always taken me to the right place before – I had no reason to believe that this time might be different.

As I got deeper and deeper into Brixton, however, I became more and more uncomfortable. I was becoming increasingly sure that Ahmed was not going to be where the map was taking me. Then the app told me that I had arrived – just as I came to Coldharbour Lane. Now, if you Google 'is Coldharbour Lane dangerous?' then you get the answer that it has been described as 'the most dangerous street in the most dangerous borough in London'. From what I could see, there was no reason to doubt this. There were four police riot vans pulled up against the curb, with a significant police presence on the street, while various groups of very criminal looking characters were loitering around. Litter and graffiti were everywhere and several of the buildings had broken windows – and if the app was right, I was probably going to have to go inside one of them.

Ahmed had given very clear delivery instructions describing his address, but I could see nothing remotely resembling them. I circled around but was becoming less and less convinced that this was – despite the map's assurances – the right place. As I cycled slowly up and down the road trying to spot something that could, at least with some imagination, fit the instructions, I could feel eyes watching me from all directions. When I passed people they seemed to stop talking and glare at me. This was probably largely my imagination, but on the other hand I had never seen such a concentration of criminal appearances. If I couldn't find Ahmed soon, and if he was anything like the people around here, I might end up getting stabbed.

At last I decided to put Ahmed's postcode into Google Maps and double check. I was both relieved and worried to see that he was indeed back in Clapham, a good two miles away: relieved because I could get back to known territory, but worried because I had already spent at least half an hour trying to find him and his food was almost certainly cold. Ahmed was going to be mad. Following Google Maps, and more than forty minutes after I should have been there, I at length reached the right place. I could see a man standing outside, obviously waiting. I hoped he hadn't been there the whole time. Fully expecting him to be justly furious, I approached him tentatively.

'Are you waiting for a Deliveroo order?'

'Yes – are you Owen?' Customers can see your first name for purposes of identification when you get there. 'I'm so pleased to see you at last!'

At least he didn't sound cross. I began to apologise profusely for the delay, explaining what had happened.

'There's no need to apologise,' he said. 'I'm sorry that you've had to go to all of this effort for me. I just imagined that you had other deliveries to do on the way.'

This was not the reception I had been expecting, but it was a welcome one. Then he started pulling out his wallet. I had no idea why he was doing it as payment is wholly made through the app, and my amazement only increased when he handed me a £5 note.

'I'm so sorry that you had this bother,' he repeated, insisting that I take it. I was immensely grateful, partly for the tip (the only cash tip that I was ever given) but mostly because he was taking it so well. He would have been entitled to be cross, even more so as when I handed over his order I could feel that it was lukewarm at best.

What was happening to me? Were all the apps trying to get me killed? Was there some conspiracy to remove me from the scene? Why had both incidents involved Brixton – did the area have an influence on navigation apps? Or was it just another example of misfortunes piling up together? At any rate, I was still alive – and able to carry on riding.

That wasn't to say I was going to let the matter drop without making some sort of statement. I might have benefited in the end with Ahmed's tip but (firstly) Deliveroo didn't know that and (secondly) it didn't alter the fact that I had wasted nearly an hour trying to find a customer because Deliveroo's software had taken me to entirely the wrong place.

I scented an opportunity to make a bit more money. It was time to put in a claim for loss of earnings.

Right from when I had signed up, I had frequently been assured that if ever I had a problem then there was a friendly rider support team ready and waiting to help. I had never needed to use this service, but I reckoned that now was as good chance as any to test it out.

The first obstruction was not long in becoming obvious. It transpired that the 24/7 support phone line was limited to immediate problems, for instance not being able to find a customer. Whilst that had indeed been my problem half an hour ago, I had managed to solve it independently. I was now comfortably back in my room and my problem was more past than immediate. There was, however, an email address which I could use. I got typing.

When I had finished, I considered my email to be a model of advocacy. It opened with an appeal to company pride as, in glowing terms, I described how much working as a Deliveroo rider was helping me through a trying time of my life. It outlined how the money I was earning was enabling me to cover all my living costs whilst the flexible hours allowed me to conveniently work around my studies. Then I started to get to the point. It was all very well being flexible, I said, but the reason I needed flexibility was because I had other things to do. I only had so much time in which to earn the money I needed. And how, I asked, could I earn enough money if Deliveroo was sending me on a wild goose chase miles from where I needed to be? In heart-wrenching terms I portrayed my increasing worry as the chilly air sucked the heat from Ahmed's lunch, and my fear of an angry reception as I got later and later.

Having set the scene, I made my claim. It was not ambitious. I hoped that at this stage of the email, whoever was reading it would be feeling desperately sorry for me so that when they saw the extent of my desire they would be sure to grant it. A humble £10 was all I asked. £8 for the wasted 40 minutes (two thirds of the £12/ hour I was told I could earn), plus £2 for the minor emotional trauma I had suffered. Surely that was reasonable by anyone's standards.

Optimistically, I sent the email and sat back to await my pay-out. At least I didn't have long to wait for a reply. Seconds later, an email popped into my inbox. It was not exactly what I wanted.

'Thanks for your feedback! Your comments will be used to improve our service in future.'

That was nice to know. On the other hand, my £10 wasn't much in evidence. I clicked reply. Whilst I was glad, I said, that other riders would hopefully avoid a similar experience to mine, that didn't alter the fact that the software had caused me to waste 40 minutes of potential earning. Could I have some compensation, please?

Again, the reply wasn't long in coming. 'Thanks for your feedback! Your comments will be used to improve our service in future.'

I gave up. At least I knew for the future how much I could expect to rely on the rider support team. I just hoped that my failure to get what I wanted wasn't a reflection on my advocacy skills. If I couldn't even get £10 out of Deliveroo then how could I expect to succeed as a barrister when much greater sums of money were at stake?

Chapter Six: More Trouble

Anyone who thinks my story is anywhere near over is sadly mistaken.

Donald Trump

The days turned into weeks, which started to turn into months. As I did more and more deliveries, the experiences began to merge into one another in my memory. Now that I had properly got the hang of the job, I was rarely fazed by any of the problems that I regularly faced. However, when difficulties did arise, like buses they tended to all arrive together.

Sometimes the problem of finding the customer didn't arise until I had arrived at roughly the right place. Delivering in London was rarely as simple as going to the house and knocking on the door; most of my customers lived in apartments or flats and expected me to take their delivery right up to them. Some of these apartment blocks had only just been built so the satnav would only take me to the approximate area, leaving me to then find the right building and entrance independently. To get into other places could require the ingenuity of a Colditz escaper. Finally, to make my job really nice and easy, it was invariably the case that the customers who left detailed delivery instructions needn't have bothered but when I needed such instructions there weren't any.

Occasionally I got an address which looked like a code, particularly if the customer hadn't bothered to put in any punctuation. Take this one, which I got one day in mid-March:

'E14 Oscar Dr Amira Mir'

To me, a humble Deliveroo rider rather than Alan Turing, this looked incomprehensible. For a start there was a complete lack of punctuation: was it supposed to be E14, Oscar, Dr Amira Mir, or E14 Oscar, Dr Amira Mir, or E14, Oscar Dr, Amira Mir? Was 'Dr' Amira Mir's title, or was it short for 'Drive'? Who or what was Oscar? And as for 'E14', that sounded more like a new sort of petrol than an address.

At any rate, as the satnav had provided a clear route to follow I decided to leave off worrying about the specifics for the moment. After what had happened in the past I had no guarantee that I would even get to the right place – there was no point stressing about the details until I had arrived.

As I passed MI5 I was momentarily distracted by the one-in-a-million sight of a man walking out of its gate wearing a sweater with the words 'I AM A SPY' emblazoned across it. *Perhaps it's an elaborate double bluff*, I pondered. After all, no terrorist suspect is going to believe that a man wearing such a jumper is actually a member of the security services. Or maybe it was just his first day on the job.

The solution to the riddle of the address turned out to be quite simple. I pedalled through a set of gates into Oscar Drive, which transpired to be a newly built estate consisting mainly of blocks of flats. The developers had obviously decided to break with all conventions: instead of numbering the buildings, they had lettered them. It didn't help that they weren't in alphabetical order; no doubt the architect had good reasons for positioning the buildings such that one passed F then D before accessing E by going behind H, but his logic was not obvious to uninitiated minds like my own.

At last, I reached E. As I stepped towards the door I could hear an irritating buzzing noise, but it soon stopped – only to start again as I pressed the button for No.14. I waited for someone to answer over the intercom but, hearing nothing, I pressed the button again. Still nothing but the buzzing. I gave up and rang the customer's number.

A cross, female voice got straight to the point. 'Where have you got to?' This was not the most encouraging thing to hear but, then again, perhaps the pangs of hunger were influencing her mood.

'I'm just outside,' I began. Hopefully, if she knew her dinner was almost on her table she might cheer up. Her next words, however, showed that the problem wasn't any concern about my whereabouts.

'I know where you are. I unlocked the door as soon as you arrived.' *Well, thanks for telling me now.* As I'm not in the habit of just pushing open people's doors without permission, I hadn't tried the door yet.

However, I took this as implied consent (as we say in law) to enter so I pushed the door. Nothing happened.

'Er, it appears to have locked again,' I ventured. The customer (presumably Amira Mir) could not have sounded more irritated if I'd said I had eaten her order. Then the buzzing started again. Finally, I realised that this was the noise the door made when unlocked. As you might imagine, by this point in time I had gained quite a lot of experience with the entrances to flats but this was not like anything I had ever heard when a door was unlocked. Normally they make a sort of click and move slightly, but this sounded more like a faulty air conditioning unit – clearly another innovation of the developers of this strange estate.

I climbed up several flights of stairs before reaching the top floor. The stairs were just wide enough for one person, terminating at a door at the top to access the landing. Now came the next problem: my bag physically could not fit around the door. The architect by now was really getting on my nerves. Thankfully a woman, whom I assumed was Amira Mir, had now come out onto the landing so I could just hand her the package without having to get through, but the expression on her face as she saw me trying to get through the door like an obese cat through a flap was not encouraging.

At last, with great relief (and not a little difficulty) I headed back down the stairs, let myself out of the door and cycled out of the gates of Oscar Drive.

As it was now approaching the end of the peak period and I had a tutorial in about an hour, I decided to head homewards but stay online in case I got offered an order which I could do in the time available. I was cruising down the Wandsworth Road through thick but fast-flowing traffic when an order popped up on my screen. It was from Pizza Hut – which I had literally just passed on the other side of the road. I don't know what came over me. I had often seen other riders executing insane manoeuvres but, even now, I tended to prioritise my safety over knocking a minute or two off the job. Up until that point I would never have considered executing a U-turn on the Wandsworth Road in this sort of traffic.

Maybe it was the faint feeling of time pressure that I didn't normally have. Or maybe the last barrier to money's ultimate prioritisation had finally disappeared. Whatever the reason was, I found myself swinging out into the middle of the road. I kept moving forwards to maintain momentum as I waited for a slight gap in the traffic. The oncoming cars were all having to move across to get past me safely. Just then, I saw a huge lorry coming on rapidly just a few vehicles down. There was no way that it was going to be able to squeeze past me, and I suspected the driver wouldn't stop either. I had to act fast. I slammed my right foot down onto the road and squeezed the back brake, dropping into first gear at the same time. My bike skidded around 180 degrees and I was racing back up the middle of the road to the accompaniment of horns from drivers on both sides of the road. I slid through the cars to the cycle lane and pulled up outside Pizza Hut.

Within a couple of minutes, I had a box of pizza in my bag and was pedalling towards Brixton down an empty bus lane. I was vaguely aware of two women walking down the pavement just ahead of me, both on their phones with headphones on. Nothing to worry about there. Suddenly they both just stepped out in front of me – not even glancing back to see if anything was coming, and with their headphones certainly unable to hear anything either. I just had time to yell a warning and swerve slightly before I smashed into the nearer one at 15mph. She screamed and staggered backwards. I was vaguely aware of her phone flying through the air alongside me. There followed a nasty crack as its screen shattered on the road and a splash as it slid through a drain grating and disappeared.

Oooops.

It had all happened so quickly that I was already a good thirty yards down the road before I had even had time to grab the brakes. I put my reflexes on hold as I briefly considered what to do. Chips were flying off my remaining stump of humanity as fast as the justifications for not stopping were rushing through my mind:

1. There was no point in stopping now, seeing that I was already so far down the road.

2. I had no intention of paying for any damage, seeing that the accident was not my fault.

3. The women would probably be shocked and angry – so telling them that I didn't intend to pay for any damage would undoubtedly create an unpleasant scene.

4. I was angry at the carelessness of the women: it didn't take a genius to conclude that stopping would be a recipe for an argument.

5. The owner of the phone ought to be grateful she'd only lost her phone – if I'd been a bus she could have been flattened.

6. I had a delivery to complete.

In conclusion, I didn't stop.

It didn't take much longer to get to the customer's house which was charmingly located backing onto Brixton Prison. That place seemed to have a magnetic influence on me. More to the immediate point, directly in front of the house was a gang of workmen busily drilling up the pavement. I really could think of nicer places to be. Hundreds of murderers locked up a few yards away and a very real risk of having my eardrums blown out by two pneumatic drills operating simultaneously.

However, my main concern was getting to the customer. I could see his door, clearly marked with the number I had been given. The only issue was that his front gate was completely obstructed by the workmen. There seemed to be little chance of persuading them to let me through even had I wanted to risk life and limb traversing the cavernous hole which they were busy enlarging in the pavement. I considered ringing the customer but realised that it would be all but impossible to hear what he was saying when I had about 200 decibels worth of pneumatic drill hammering away a couple of yards away. I had to get more creative.

The neighbours' front gate was free from any obstructions. It would be easy to go into their patch of front garden, get over the fence and into the customer's garden. There was a snag: this would technically be trespass (not a crime, I know, but I could get sued), and there were five witnesses standing in the road. Two of them were occupied with their drills but the other three were apparently just there for moral support, in the way of builders all over the country. They had pocketed their phones and lit cigarettes while they watched with interest the Deliveroo rider wheeling his bike back and forth like a mechanical toy.

Never mind. This was Brixton, after all, and surely the men had seen people climbing over fences before. Therefore, I locked up my bike and entered the neighbouring property. I made my way to the fence. It wasn't too high so I was able to scramble over it easily into the customer's garden, using my usual technique of acting as if I was perfectly entitled to be doing what I was (in the circumstances, this was more difficult than usual, but at least I wasn't trying to get in through a window).

The next problem was communicating with the customer that I had arrived. I had already decided that phoning was out of the question. There was a small knocker on the door but there was unsurprisingly no response when I tried it, bearing in mind the noise behind me. My only remaining option was to beat a thunderous tattoo on the door with both fists, which eventually succeeded in attracting someone's attention. The door opened. I assumed the man was saying hello – his mouth opened and shut like a goldfish but I could hear nothing except the racket behind me.

"I've got your Deliveroo order!" I roared at the top of my voice, but the words were snatched away like a leaf in a November storm. Anticipating that he would be unable to hear me, I matched actions to words by opening my bag and producing a package of food with a flourish, like a rabbit from a top hat.

"Thank you," the man mouthed as he took the order. There was obviously no point in prolonging the conversation but, despite having waved goodbye, I waited until he had shut the door before taking the same unorthodox method of departure that I had used on the way in. I gave a cheery thumbs-up to the workmen, who were still watching me with interest as I came out of the neighbour's gate. I hoped they were impressed with my innovation.

Then, with my ears still ringing, it was back to the dreariness of study in my bedroom. As I sat there, grappling with the finer points of contract law in the virtual atmosphere of Microsoft Teams, my mind was still out in the wilds of London. It was a world away, in more ways than one.

I was living parallel lives in two worlds which were both, whatever I pretended to myself, becoming increasingly nightmarish. Deliveroo might provide a welcome break from my studies but part of me was starting to recognise that I didn't really enjoy dicing with death on a daily basis on London's streets, to say nothing of breaking people's phones or having to puzzle my way into a range of less pleasant buildings.

There was another world available to me. One without the constant roar of traffic and difficult customers but nonetheless one which was very much in real life. One where my food would be cooked for me and I would have other people constantly around me…

I banished such thoughts from my mind. I had come so far now that I wasn't going to give up early. Home was for the holidays.

Chapter Seven: It Takes All Sorts

Caught between a rock and a hard place.

English idiom

Shortly afterwards I was assigned to what was far and away the biggest order I ever carried. It was from Waitrose (Deliveroo was into grocery deliveries long before the recent explosion of the likes of Weezy, Zapp, Getir, etc.) to one Adam Johns, living in a brand-new apartment block near Battersea Park. When I arrived at the shop I was given an enormous bag which I had to strain to lift. I managed to fit it into my bag – and then, to my horror, was given another one equally as big. Somehow, I squeezed them both in (requiring some major stretching of the seams) and heaved my bag onto my back. I lurched out of the shop, slightly concerned that the weight would give me curvature of the spine such that I would spend the rest of my life looking at the sky.

When I started cycling, I was weighted down so much at the back that I unintentionally did a wheelie. Thankfully, the journey was all downhill; I rocketed down one hill at a speed which I am not likely to attain on a bike again. Upon arrival, however, I found that what I had gained on the swings I was about to lose on the roundabouts: I had to go up to the seventh floor to get to my customer's apartment. At least there was a lift – seven flights of stairs would have been beyond me. I staggered into the lift, wondering if it would be able to cope with this sort of weight in it. My face was red with exertion as I reached Mr Johns' door. Gasping for breath, I dropped the bag with a thud onto the landing. The feeling as my back lost the strain was incredible – I felt like I was about to float up to the ceiling. I grinned as I imagined Mr Johns opening the door to find me hovering around the ceiling like an enormous butterfly. However, my feet remained planted on terra firma as I knocked on the door.

This being so, Mr Johns, a standard-looking man in his mid-thirties, did not seem to see anything extraordinary in getting a cyclist to deliver an order which would have been more suitable for a van. I asked him in a tone of studied politeness if he wanted a hand with the second enormous bag, but he didn't seem to take the hint. He just thanked me briefly and said goodbye. I headed for the lift, sarcastically telling myself how nice it was to feel that my hard work had been truly appreciated. At least I hadn't suffered any permanent damage.

The following morning I woke up to find to find a thick layer of snow on the ground. When I turned on my phone, I found that Deliveroo was offering huge bonuses to all riders who went out and, what's more, the app was showing the area to be busy at what is normally the quietest time of the week. The money was tempting but, for the first time in a while, I let common sense have the final say: a bit of cash wasn't worth the risk of having a serious injury. I was prepared to accept muggers as an occupational hazard; Mother Nature, however, was (at least in my view) a far more dangerous foe.

When I went out for a walk a bit later, I looked in through the window of Starbucks and saw a line of orders waiting to be collected – but no riders. It was obvious that customers had woken up and decided it was the moment for some comfort food, and equally obvious that the riders had all woken up and sensibly decided not to work. I wouldn't have been surprised if some of those customers didn't get their delivery for a couple of hours at least.

By the end of the week, however, the snow had all gone and I decided to make up for lost time, notwithstanding that the thermometer was reading minus 9°C and the ponds on Clapham Common were frozen solid. My four layers of clothing seemed to be on the verge of giving up the struggle to ward off the chilly breeze when an order popped up from a small coffee shop/ bakery nearby. I was instantly attracted by the fact that I would earn £6 for the delivery, as the customer was more than three miles away in Dulwich. As I followed the directions toward the bakery, I was wondering what sort of order she would have: I imagined it would be a decent-sized package in order to make the huge delivery fee worthwhile.

I was rather taken aback, therefore, when I arrived and was handed the grand total of one tuna sandwich. Admittedly, it was a nice-looking bakery, but I wasn't convinced a) that it was an appropriate meal for the weather or b) that it was appropriate to spend that much money on such a small delivery. In the time it took me to get to the bakery, pick up the sandwich, and get to the customer, she could have made a dozen sandwiches and eaten them. Furthermore, she must have spent at least £15 (once you factor in my wage, Deliveroo's cut of the price, and the cost of the sandwich) when she could have bought the ingredients for a week's worth of sandwiches for less than a pound.

Anyway, it wasn't for me to judge her. Maybe she was trying to support local (local?) independent businesses or had some equally worthy goal in mind. Swinging my leg over the saddle, I began to peddle carefully through the icy streets. When, at last, I arrived, my hands were so numb that I couldn't undo the zip on my bag. The woman watched me with increasing sympathy as I wrestled with it for what seemed an age. After I had finally got it open, given her the package and was cycling away, a message popped up to inform me that she had given me a retrospective tip. I could only wish that more customers were as sympathetic – but by that point she must have paid about three times the cost of the sandwich on the delivery.

Having completed that order, I was cycling around aimlessly waiting to be assigned to another job when the sudden blare of sirens made me jump. Six police riot vans, each crammed with policemen, raced past me in tight convoy.

Now I have this strange sensation that comes over me when I see lots of emergency vehicles together that makes me follow them to see what is happening. I don't know why this is as I wouldn't describe myself as an adrenalin junkie. The fact remains that, as I had nothing else to do, I swung out behind the vans in pursuit.

I didn't have far to go. They had all pulled to a halt just down the road and were disgorging police in full riot gear. I slowed down to look around but couldn't see anything. Then more police, including mounted police, came streaming across from the park bordering the road. I was intrigued: whatever could be happening? Getting off my bike, I started walking into the park to find out what was going on.

My feet had barely touched the grass when I heard cheering. Lots of it. My eyes traced the sound to a mass of people coming through the park at a fast walk; there must have been thousands of them, pouring through the park, waving placards. From the messages they displayed, I realised that this was an anti-lockdown protest – and not a particularly peaceful one either. That's not to say that the protestors had felt constrained to limit themselves to one theme. Alongside the 'Freedom from Restrictions' type placards, there were anti-abortion ones, Donald Trump 'Make America Great Again' banners, and all sorts. At first, I found this quite funny. Then I looked behind me. A thick blue line of policemen in full riot gear had surrounded the park and were closing in. I turned again. The protestors were pouring towards the police, shouting defiance. And I was in the middle. I realised that, within about 30 seconds, I was going to be the jam in this delightful sandwich. Not having any desire to either get arrested or get my bike damaged, I decided that it was probably safest to move towards the police – who had now cordoned off the entire park with a wall of shields. The Kevlar just needed replacing by armour to complete the image of a pack of berserk Ancient Britons surrounded by unflinching Roman legionaries.

The police seemed to be setting up to kettle the protestors, and spending the next few hours penned in with a rabid crowd was not my idea of a fun afternoon. It was high time to get to a safer spot. Pushing my bike towards the oncoming legion, I was slightly apprehensive as to whether they would force me to stay in the park but, thankfully, they moved aside to allow me to walk through their cordon. This done, I stopped to watch what would happen.

I had been only just in time. The two armies clashed viciously. Led by a modern Boadicea, the protestors charged the wall of shields, bellowing like a herd of stampeding cattle. The cohorts collapsed into confusion as the mob came off victorious, getting through to the road with banners waving jubilantly. It was at this point, though, that the cavalry arrived in the shape of another convoy of police vans packed with reinforcements. They skidded to a halt right by the action as policemen poured out of them to join the fray.

This time they were able to pen the protestors in properly. History was repeating itself as overall victory went to the Imperial Roman Army's police replacement.

Now that the excitement was mostly over, the press was starting to arrive. Cameramen were climbing fences to get footage of the contained chaos whilst reporters were firing questions at other bystanders. Not without regret, as it was an interesting spectacle, I decided that it would be prudent to leave – I did not want to have my face in the news as connected with a violent protest for fear that it might have an impact on my career.

As I got nearer home, I started to get an uncomfortable feeling that I was being followed. The mix-up with the riot had kept me out longer than I had anticipated, and the light was beginning to fade. I noticed a cyclist behind me. Although I would always beat him away from traffic lights, he would invariably then catch up with me – but he never tried to overtake. I would hear his heavy breathing a couple of yards behind me, until the next time I could accelerate ahead from traffic lights. I wasn't particularly concerned about his intentions but didn't really like the idea of someone following me all the way home. It could have been entirely coincidental but, as he stuck behind me through another turning, I began to wonder what he was up to.

I decided I would at least work out whether he was in fact following me. If he was, then I would take steps to throw him off – quickly, too, as we were now approaching where I would be turning off to get home. He was still puffing along just behind me.

Suddenly, without signalling or braking, I shot off the road, through an alleyway, and into a residential street. As I did so, I heard the squeal of brakes behind me as the man came to grips with this unexpected manoeuvre. There was a slight pause – then the silhouette of a cyclist appeared between the walls of the alley.

This seemed to indicate that he was indeed on my tail. Very well. The odds were on my side. From the last couple of months' experiences, I reckoned that I knew the surrounding warren of alleys and backstreets better than most people alive. Even if he knew them just as well, he was going to need a lot of foresight to predict where I had gone. The game was on.

I accelerated hard. He might be faster than me on the straight but round these estates he wouldn't have a chance to get up to speed. I could have wished I was a little less distinctive with my big bag on, but I wasn't going to leave it behind. It just meant he had a bit more of a chance of seeing where I had gone.

He was still behind me. I smiled. A small cul-de-sac opened on the right. I shot down it. At the end, a footpath led off to the left. As I flew down it my peripheral vision clocked my follower turning down the cul-de-sac.

Just then a piercing scream rang out ahead, followed by a heart-rending sob. My nerves, already tight with the excitement of the chase, twanged like a banjo string. I shot desperate glances from side to side, fully expecting to be embroiled in a brutal crime, only to see a fox step leisurely out into the footpath. At least I didn't have to worry about someone being murdered. I swerved around it and dived down another footpath on the right. Straight across a narrow street, left through an alley, up a short hill, along a couple more streets, and I was nearly home. I took a quick circuit around the block to make sure that I really had lost the man before pulling to a halt and drawing a deep breath.

The icy air had been forgotten in the thrill of the afternoon's events but now, as I unlocked the garage door, the chill caught up with me again. I put my bike away, headed up to my room, and awarded myself a long, relaxing hot chocolate.

With some surprise, I realised that it was nearly the end of term. The last few months had been challenging, but Deliveroo had provided me with an escape route (albeit often making it feel like I was just getting out of the frying pan to jump straight into the fire). Now I could start thinking about going home for Easter – and forget all about Deliveroo for a while.

***

A couple of days later I was sitting in Paddington Station waiting for the train that would take me home. Home: away from the dismal streets of London in lockdown; away from the depressing virtual world of Microsoft Teams; away from the job which had saved me and almost shattered me in the process. I was wearing one of my Deliveroo T-shirts – comfortable, hard-wearing, and a badge of achievement.

My platform was announced and I made my way to the ticket barrier. Exhausted from ten weeks of living and working in two nightmare worlds, I sank back into my seat and closed my eyes. For the first time in those ten weeks, I felt truly relaxed. I was going home. I could hardly believe it. No need to worry about whether I would yet again be the only student to participate in an online tutorial. No need to worry about whether I would yet again have to deal with knife-wielding muggers or impossible entry systems. I was going home.

Slowly, almost imperceptibly, the train began to move. Moments later, it was already out of the station, smoothly, effortlessly, gathering speed. No traffic lights to slow it down. No internet glitches to end its connection to what had almost begun to feel like reality. The rocking of the train as we reached maximum operating speed lulled me to sleep.

It felt like I had hardly closed my eyes when the train began to slow down. My station was announced.

'Please ensure that you take all your belongings with you and take care when stepping down from the train. Thank you for travelling with Great Western Railway.'

That announcement had never sounded so good. I looked out of the window. I could see my parents' car pulling into the station car park. I was home.

Then I noticed a moped driving along the road parallel to the railway line, its rider wearing an unmistakeable jacket. I looked down at the logo on my T-shirt. It was the same.

Deliveroo had followed me home.

Epilogue: Into the Sunset

Never take anything for granted.

Benjamin Disraeli

My final and in many ways most bizarre experience with Deliveroo occurred not in London but in my local town. I had seen a Deliveroo rider as my train pulled into the station, bringing me home for Easter; the company had obviously come to the town, and after the last few months' experience in London I thought it would be interesting to give it a go elsewhere. Therefore, once my exams had finished in May, I brought my bag home with me. In fact, I found myself too busy to do it much, but one warm Friday evening I felt full of energy and, as the app was saying it was busy, I got my bike out and headed into town.

I soon found delivering in a smallish town to be a very different kettle of fish to what I'd been experiencing for the past few months in London. There, every customer and the place where they lived had been unique while almost every delivery had posed a challenge of some sort. Here, on the other hand, everyone to whom I delivered seemed to be Mr Normal living in a normal house. No apartment blocks to enter, no muggers en route; all I had to do was knock on the door and wait to be greeted by a smiling customer. I felt how I imagine soldiers must feel returning from a combat zone for training – it was easy to the point of being boring.

Then things started to get a little more interesting. I accepted an order from Nando's, which would pay me £5.17. This sounded great, particularly as the customer's location didn't look too far away. Not only was the job easy, but it also seemed like the pay was getting better as well.

Minutes later I arrived at the restaurant and headed round to the back entrance. I pushed open the door and entered. The kitchen was empty but I could see movement through a connecting door which led to the counter. After a brief wait, a woman appeared through the door. She smiled a greeting.

'Hi, I'm here for order 1642,' I told her brightly.

She went through into a side-room and examined a row of three packages. 'Which number, sorry?' she asked. '1543?'

'No, 1642,' I confirmed after checking my screen.

'Can I see what it contains? It doesn't seem to be here.'

Thinking that she would perhaps be able to compile the order from my list, I brought it up and showed her: a grilled peri-peri chicken wrap and some boneless chicken thighs.

'Ah,' she said. 'I remember. The customer picked that up herself more than an hour ago.'

I was somewhat taken aback. Fair enough if the customer wanted to pick up their own order, but why had I then been assigned to deliver it more than an hour later?

The woman gave me a conspiratorial wink. 'Doesn't stop you making the money though, does it?' She grinned broadly. 'Just say you've collected it and make some easy money.'

The job was getting easier and easier. 'Fair enough,' I chuckled, and turned to go. I clicked 'collected order' and headed back to where I had left my bike. As soon as the app would let me, I 'completed the delivery'. I had got £5 for doing practically nothing and was now ready for another order. *If only it had been like this in London*, I thought contentedly. *I could make a career out of this*.

That was when I was assigned to pick up a Co-op order consisting of a multipack of cans of lager and a box of chocolates. Nothing particularly unusual there – even if it wasn't exactly a stereotypical Deliveroo order. I collected the order with no difficulty and was shortly pedalling off to 8, Sycamore Street, which sounded like just another standard house. I expected I would then hand over the order to the customer – a Rob Wainwright, who sounded just like yet another Mr Normal – and be on my way.

Within five minutes I was dismounting outside a large, detached house with a Jaguar parked on the drive. *A bit different to the sort of places I usually deliver to in London, but certainly no cause for complaint*, I thought. Blissfully unaware of what awaited me, I rang the bell. A tall, thin, middle-aged man opened the door.

'Good evening,' I greeted him breezily. 'Here's your order. Because it contains alcohol, could I ask to see…' My voice died away as I saw him looking at me with the sort of detached, sympathetic, slightly disgusted expression one might have when shown a picture of a chimpanzee with some debilitating disease.

'I haven't ordered anything.'

'Oh!' This was a bit of a surprise but I kept my composure. 'Are you sure? This is 8, Sycamore Street, isn't it? That's what it says here: 4 cans of lager and a box of chocolates for Rob Wainwright at 8, Sycamore Street.'

'That's this address,' he was forced to concede. 'But I've never heard that name before. What's more, I'm diabetic, and I never touch lager, let alone the Deliveroo app. There must be a mistake somewhere.' Thank goodness Sherlock Holmes was there to join up the dots with an unfathomable leap of logic.

Noticing that the ratio of sympathy to disgust on his face was definitely swinging in an unfavourable direction, I decided I would leave him alone.

'If that's the case, I'm terribly sorry for disturbing you. I'll ring the number provided and try to sort it out. Have a lovely evening.'

He instantly brightened at the prospect of my impending departure. ‘No worries. I hope you get it sorted.’ With that, he shut the door. I walked back to the pavement and dialled Rob’s number. A voice answered warily.

‘Hello… who is it?’

Back to my breezy, self-assured tone. ‘Hello, is that Rob? I’ve got your Deliveroo order here.’

He became enthusiastic. ‘Splendid! I’ll be right down, won’t be a minute.’

‘Er, well, the fact is, I’ve just been to the address you’ve given, and they don’t know anything about you.’

This didn’t seem an enormous surprise to him. He chuckled. ‘What number does it say?’

‘Eight.’

‘Ha, ha, ha!’ he guffawed. ‘Well, well, well! No wonder they didn’t know me! What a stupid mistake! I live at Number 7, just across the road.’

Rather a strange mistake to make, I thought, a*nd surely the people across the road know who lives opposite? Never mind, this will soon be sorted*. ‘OK then, I’ll see you in just a minute.’

He paused. ‘Actually, I’m out at the moment but my brother’s in. I’ll text him to tell him you’re coming over.’ This was a bit of a contradiction of what he’d said at the start of the conversation, but I decided to ignore it. As long as someone was in to take the stuff, they could be his brother, boss, or a burglar for all it mattered to me. I ended the call, headed across the road, and knocked on Number 7's door. A blonde woman of indeterminate age opened it. She obviously wasn't Rob's brother but, given his muddle over his address, he might well have got his siblings confused too. Nevertheless, I was reasonably confident that she wasn't anything to do with Rob either. I decided to play it safe.

'Good evening, is Rob around?' I wasn't going to make the mistake again of assuming that the person at the address was going to be expecting an order.

'Rob… which Rob? No one called Rob lives here.' *Surprise, surprise.*

'Rob Wainwright – he's ordered a Deliveroo to here.' I explained about my visit to Number 8 and subsequent phone call.

'Well, I don't know anything about it. Sorry.' She said goodbye and closed the door. I redialled Rob's number wondering where on earth I would be sent next, and to how many other random people I would have to apologise for disturbing their evenings.

He was obviously expecting the call. 'Success?' he enquired brightly.

'No, *she* didn't know anything about you either,' I said, emphasising the 'she'.

He didn't seem to notice the reference to the identity of the person who was supposed to be at Number 7. His next statement, however, soon put that minor detail firmly in the shade.

'I'm actually in the USA right now.' *Wow! I've only just left Sherlock Holmes at Number 8 and now I'm talking to Superman who's managed to cross the Atlantic in under five minutes*. My mind was beginning to boggle.

'Go on,' I said. My cynicism was plain. Was he going to tell me he'd booked me a flight to the States to give him the order? A Deliveroo trans-Atlantic business trip must have been unparalleled.

'Don't worry, you're at the right address. I don't know why they said they don't know me' – *you might not, but I've got a pretty good idea,* I thought – 'but go back to Number 7 and tell them it's a present from Rob. Tell them, Rob says hi. Then your job is done, I promise.'

This was obviously nonsense but I decided to give it a go anyway. So back I went to Number 7.

'Sorry, it's me again. I've been on the phone to Rob again, and he said to give you this package and say hi to you from him.' I felt like a right nincompoop as she stared disbelievingly at me.

'Well, I can assure you that I have never heard of him.' This was getting ridiculous. If I didn't do something about it, we could go back and forth like this all night. I decided to force the proceedings on a touch.

'Rob's just told me that he's in America,' I said persuasively, 'so there's no way he wants this stuff himself. I don't want it. Why don't you have it anyway? Some lager, some chocolates... Treat yourself,' I encouraged her.

Maybe I should consider a career as a salesman. Or maybe the free food spoke for itself. After all, lager and chocolates don't blow in through the door every day. Whatever the reason, she took the package. With an immense feeling of satisfaction, I ticked 'Delivery Complete.' I considered ringing Rob again to give him a message of thanks from his brother but decided to leave him hanging. He had obviously just ordered to a random address, but it seemed like a bizarre prank to me – not only had he spent a total of around £25 (according to my calculations) on the order, but all that he got out of it was a couple of phone calls.

Heading back to my bike, I logged out of the app for what turned out to be the last time. As I cycled home in the warm summer evening, I didn't think that this would be the case; Rob certainly hadn't frightened me out of riding again. However, I didn't know then that other things would intervene; that by the time I headed back to London in the autumn my university course would finally be being taught in-person; or that by then I would have earned enough money from other jobs to see me through until the next summer.

All I knew then was that the beautiful June sunset over the Oxfordshire countryside was a million miles from my first ride. The wind and sleet of that January afternoon in London were just a dim and distant memory as I got home and had a shower to cool off rather than warm up. I had put down my bag for the final time – and, many months later, I would pick up my pen.

Appendix One: Reflections

It's a funny old world.

Margaret Thatcher

The concept behind riding for Deliveroo could hardly be simpler: cycle – collect – cycle – deliver. What's more, nine times out of ten when I was doing it in my local town that was precisely how easy it was. In London, however, that statistic could be reversed without any exaggeration. Nine times out of ten there was some snag that transformed what should be one of the easiest jobs on the planet into one of the hardest.

My time working for (for? with?) Deliveroo in London provided a range of experiences which I wouldn't have missed for anything. It also got me cold, wet, and tired on innumerable occasions, took me to some very dodgy places, and led to some close shaves. Was it worth it? Definitely. Would I do it again? Maybe... not. I do not miss it at all. This might sound strange bearing in mind the stories I have just been recounting but I would explain it by saying that, to my mind at least, it is inextricably linked with the horrors of studying online, alone, in my bedroom for months on end. I still have my kit but have not even considered going out again since I started having in-person teaching (nearly half-way through my degree).

The six months during which I worked as a Deliveroo rider (January to June 2021) provided an educational experience, the lessons from which have had a lasting impact on me. Educational? Certainly not regarding the work itself. Taking food from restaurants to houses was hardly mentally stimulating; I doubt I gained one new neural connection from clicking 'Accept Order' on however many occasions. However, while I was doing it, I learnt quite a lot about myself and other people. It must be one of the few things where the beneficial side-effects outweigh the intrinsic benefits.

What did I learn about myself? I saw life at its best and worst, richest and poorest, safest and most dangerous. From the luxury of customers lazily awaiting dinner delivered to their door to the exhaustion of the workers frantically preparing hundreds of such meals; from the mansions of the rich to the sheds of the poor; from the security of a concierge at reception to the exposure to muggers on the streets – I saw it all. I am very thankful to have escaped unscathed: things could easily have been far worse on many occasions. I am also glad that I was able to see how 'the other half lives' at both ends of the spectrum – I visited the homes of people from practically the entire range of economic classes, and, interestingly, did not feel out of place in any of them.

More generally, I now know Clapham and Battersea like the backs of my hands and can find my way around the backstreets of Brixton, Dulwich, Kennington, and Vauxhall. Invaluable knowledge which I am probably never going to require again.

On the other hand, it's not all happy memories. For example, while riding, I on occasion willingly broke the Highway Code. While that is not something of which I am proud, though, it did provide confirmation of the fact that the rules are there for a reason. I am not, unlike, apparently, most cyclists, now addicted to infringing them. That was a lesson well learnt, which perhaps other cyclists would do well to learn too for the general good of mankind.

A sad reflection on the places that I visited in London is that while there are so many words that could be used to describe them – houses, apartments, flats, mansions – but, barring one or two exceptions, 'homes' could not be placed on the list. I increasingly felt as I went in and out of hundreds of residences that London was a place to live, not a home. I can't put my finger on it but I'm sure that there was something lacking in most places; something which, when it was occasionally present, I instantly felt it but even then would not have been able to describe it – something which transformed the humblest or grandest building into a home. Whatever it was, feeling its absence made me appreciate having a home of my own to which I could return in a way which I never had before.

Interestingly, in my local town I found that a significantly greater proportion of the houses to which I delivered felt like homes. I would be the first to admit that it cannot be a particularly nice place to live but the fact remains that the individual residences I visited felt far more homely than those in London. I don't think it was because they were closer to my own home; I think it more likely that the people who live in London do so for temporary convenience whereas those living in smaller towns are willing to make a longer commute to work having found a place to put down roots, and where they have put more effort into making a permanent home. Again, only after coming to this conclusion have I truly appreciated the stability of living in the same home for my entire life.

Overall, therefore, I got to know myself better and, whilst I have some regrets, I think in general my experiences were beneficial if only by making me appreciate my own privileges.

What about other people? It's not just customers with whom one interacts while out riding. Every day, one encounters restaurant workers, other riders, and other road users.

If you were to ask someone who drives in London regularly what they thought of Deliveroo riders, they would probably say that they are a menace to civilised road users. This, in my opinion, is a fully justified complaint. My occasional infringements of the Highway Code are nothing to what I have seen other riders doing, from jumping red lights at busy crossroads to cycling around after dark with no lights at imminent risk of being hit by even the wariest driver.

This is not to say that Deliveroo riders are alone in riding badly. On the contrary, if I had to rank the different sorts of people who ride around London it would go something like this:

1. Commuters with helmets, lights, and fluorescent clothing (best)
2. Commuters with no helmets, lights, or fluorescent clothing
3. Delivery riders
4. 'Boris bikers'
5. Electric scooter riders (absolute worst)

'Boris bikers' and electric scooter riders are the bane of all civilised cyclists' lives, as well as a growing threat to civilisation generally. The former, probably because they don't own a bike, seem to have no idea of how it is acceptable to cycle. On the pavements, off the pavements, all over the road, with no helmet or reflective clothing, I'm surprised there aren't more accidents. There are some. I saw one once: a Boris biker cycled the wrong way down a cycle lane after dark and unsurprisingly crashed into a poor, innocent commuter going the right way.

As for electric scooters, they are a plague. Whoever legalised them must have either never walked around London or taken leave of their senses. I can't even accept their legalisation as a warped practical joke. They hurtle around at insane speeds, breaching every relevant provision of the Highway Code. The reason why is obvious when you think about it: to want to ride one you must be too lazy to cycle, which means that you would prefer to use a motor, but all other motor vehicles require a licence to drive. In other words, as the people who ride electric scooters have been unable to get a licence to drive a proper vehicle, it is unsurprising that they ride badly; you can assume that they have failed a driving test somewhere along the line. These criticisms may seem like gross stereotyping; I consider them to be more like invariable rules. No doubt there are some considerate electric scooter riders out there. I have yet to come across one.

Electric bikes are also a growing phenomenon. I haven't put them in my ranking because it's hard to know where they should go. They are certainly better than electric scooters, but they are also often ridden in a highly dangerous fashion. On the other hand, there is something ludicrous about them. Once when I was cycling home, not at my top speed but I certainly wasn't hanging around, I heard a whirring noise coming up behind me and an enormously fat woman sailed past me, effortlessly pedalling along at about double my speed. I couldn't help choking with laughter as she powered down the road.

The government wants to encourage more cycling allegedly for two reasons: to reduce pollution and to make the roads safer. The second reason, in my opinion, is absurd: I feel far safer around cars than I do around other cyclists and scooterists. Other cyclists terrify me. I think, if the government really wants to make central London car-free, it should at least introduce a riding test for electric scooters and electric bikes in car-free areas.

Instead of doing this, the government is apparently trying to encourage cycling by other means. I was on more than one occasion stopped by a man offering a free on-the-spot bike service in a workshop located in a grimy bridge archway. It was funded by the government, so he said, to encourage more people to cycle. It didn't help that the man was rather rude. On the three times he tried to entice me to accept the service he leapt out in front of me while I was waiting at the traffic lights by the bridge. When I refused he demanded to know why not.

'I'd rather just do it myself, thanks,' I answered politely. I did not think it would be tactful to say that nothing would persuade me to hand over my bike to a stranger who had just stepped out from under a dark bridge and invited me to follow him back there.

'Oh,' he sneered. 'Some people just know it all, don't they?'

'That's not what I said,' I responded. 'But if I can't do anything, I'd rather pay for a service at a proper bike shop.'

Even if he was genuine, the logic of the initiative seems fatally flawed: the government doesn't seem to realise that the only people affected by it are already cycling – nobody who is not already cycling will know anything about it and thus will hardly be inspired to start.

Other road users aren't the only hazard, though. Another is the weather. I don't mind getting cold and wet if I know that I can get warm and dry when I get home, but that doesn't change the fact that it can be highly dangerous cycling in such conditions. One's stopping distance is spectacularly altered: my bike has road tires with practically no grip which means that when I slam on the brakes on a wet road I can skid for several yards before stopping. When one is in heavy traffic that can lead to some dicey situations. Meanwhile, wet drain covers can be lethal particularly when one is going round a corner – it's easy to slide sideways across them, which is not a pleasant sensation especially when one is top-heavy with a big order.

Moving back to other people that one encounters – or doesn't encounter – I imagine that non-customers wonder what is so amazing about being delivered mediocre tasting, lukewarm takeaways when one could easily cook a far tastier, healthier, and cheaper meal well within the time it will take to arrive. I certainly ponder that myself. On the other hand, customers would probably say that riders are useful because they will bring you anything.

Occasionally I came across a nice customer. Their rarity made them even more precious. On one occasion the customer was waiting outside his house to greet me. I pulled up, panting from the effort of going up a steep hill with my heavy bag.

‘You ought to get yourself a moped, mate. You’ll tire yourself out, just on a pushbike like that,’ he advised me cheerfully. I explained that I was not a full-time rider and was just doing it to earn some money and get out of the house as I was stuck with my university course being online.

‘Good on you, mate!’ he congratulated me. ‘Not many youngsters like that these days!’

On the other hand, most customers just seem to treat riders like robots, merely saying an insincere ‘thank you’ before closing the door, while a vocal minority are plain rude. I wonder how many of them are aware of what goes on behind the scenes: how hard, and in what conditions, multiple people have been working to get the food from A to B as quickly as possible.

Perhaps I shouldn’t be the only one reflecting on what I’ve been doing. Not to put too fine a point on it.

Appendix Two: Deliveroo and Editions

No matter what you do, somebody always imputes meaning into your books.

Dr Seuss

Finally, then, the big question: Editions. How many people are aware of what Deliveroo Editions is? 42% of the orders I completed as a rider came from Editions. In commerce that's (usually) a controlling share. Deliveroo's claim that it is supporting small businesses by giving them another avenue of trade seems laudable – but the truth is that it is quietly killing such businesses via Editions' 'dark kitchens' which cater for (if my experience was representative) nearly half of Deliveroo's customers.

I don't know enough about the specific details to be able to say what the exact arrangements are. All I know is that if you think you are ordering from Shake Shack, say, or another established brand, but the address is an industrial estate somewhere, you're unlikely to be getting what you think you are. It will have been cooked up in a warehouse. It may be that Editions is acting as a sort of outlet store for these brands but, as far as I'm aware, the meals are cooked from scratch in the warehouses. I would be interested to know how much the brands concerned know about what is going on.

As for the working conditions inside these 'restaurants', they may have reformed them since I was riding a year or two ago. I can say without any exaggeration that when I was visiting them in early 2021 I was appalled by what was going on there. Some of them were better. Some of them were worse. All of them were hard at work to take custom away from proper restaurants and give it to Deliveroo.

A very brief conversation I had at the Heliport industrial estate warehouse summed up the situation succinctly. It was the second or third time I had been there and I was waiting inside for my order when a lorry driver entered, apparently delivering more ingredients. He was a tough-looking, heavily tattooed character with a crew cut, but was clearly shocked at what he was seeing. I caught his eye; I could fully sympathise with what he was feeling.

'Man, this is *crazy* in here,' he muttered to me. At least, it sounded like a mutter, but given the noise around us, he'd probably had to say it quite loudly.

'You can say that again,' I agreed heartfeltly.

The last time I went there as a rider the arrangements had changed. Riders no longer had to go inside: instead, a hatch had been installed so that we could speak to a worker who would pass over the order while we remained outside. This undoubtedly made things easier for us. It also meant that we didn't – couldn't – see what was going on inside. I had to wonder whether they were getting worried about word leaking out. This suspicion has grown since I have gone back to the various warehouses in the course of writing this book and found that none of them now require riders to go inside.

Needless to say, Deliveroo paints a very different picture for its customers. If you visit the 'Editions' section on its website, you get the impression that Editions consists of self-employed chefs setting up family-run businesses. There are pictures of smiling people standing in front of Deliveroo logos with glowing descriptions of 'a community-tailored collection of restaurants' and a 'gold standard of food delivery'. One has to wonder which 'restaurants' the authors of such words had in mind.

Deliveroo is doing extraordinarily well for itself. Its riders are ubiquitous in every town of any size throughout the British Isles – but none of those riders are officially its employees. This oddity is explained when you realise this classification is saving them literally hundreds of millions of pounds of tax every year. If riders were employees then the company's whole business model would probably collapse due to the amount of tax that they would have to start paying. What, though, is the reality? In June 2021, the UK Court of Appeal held that Deliveroo riders are indeed self-employed, a material factor in the decision being that riders are not obliged to provide services personally. By contrast, in February 2021 the UK Supreme Court ruled that Uber, which has a very similar business model to Deliveroo, had to provide its taxi drivers with employment rights such as the minimum wage.

I have the greatest respect for the Court of Appeal but as far as I am aware none of its members have ever worked as a Deliveroo rider. Without wanting to sound too cocky, I have, and I think that Deliveroo riders should count as employees. This is not to say that at present, the situation justifies such a conclusion. Deliveroo has put an enormous amount of effort into ensuring that its riders are classifiable as self-employed rather than employees. It just feels like we *should* be employees, whatever the facts of the situation might appear to be.

The consequences of defining riders as self-employed are very significant, both for the company and the riders. The company saves millions in tax while the riders get no employment benefits such as the minimum wage, holiday pay, or sick pay. To me, it is obvious that the idea is a massive tax avoidance scheme which Deliveroo has been working on improving for some time. For example, until a couple of years ago, riders were paid a flat hourly rate with a bonus for every order completed. Now, however, they are paid on an order-by-order basis. This makes the 'self-employed' idea much more credible – but, on average, it has also led to riders earning less per hour. This, in turn, suggests that Deliveroo is making more money now as I don't think it's suffered from a drop in orders. The underlying substance of the situation – that the company is making a fat pile of cash from the riders who are undeniably an integral part of their business model – suggests that HMRC could do worse than to put a few questions to Deliveroo.

How should I conclude? By singing the praises of Deliveroo, or condemning it? It's certainly not an inspiring career – but it's far better than no job at all. I would recommend that all active-bodied unemployed people should sign up as Deliveroo riders (or indeed for any other similar company). I consider it would be undeniably better on economical, moral, and health-related grounds for such people to be out actually earning money than sitting on the sofa under the beneficent hand of the Welfare State.

And if you are a student who is looking for exercise, money, and flexibility, with the bonus of daily excitement and a plethora of stories to tell, I can recommend nothing better than signing up as a Deliveroo rider. All you need is a bike, a phone, and, ideally, a not too panicky temperament. Why not?

Afterword

I will have achieved my aim in writing this if any readers who use Deliveroo afterwards think more carefully about using it. I am by no means advocating avoiding it: I am all for companies with a successful business model to benefit from their efforts. What I have tried to do is present the other side of the story – the side which few people see but which is the backbone of Deliveroo's service – in order for people to know what happens between them placing their order and its arrival on their doorstep.

Finally, I owe a big thank you to Josiah Shields, without whom this book would never have been written. I'm not sure why (apart from the foreword), but that's what he wanted me to say. To be fair, his extensive feedback has been invaluable. He, or anybody else who has had anything to do with the creation of this book (including myself), may be responsible for any remaining mistakes.

O.P.

September 2022

Printed in Great Britain
by Amazon

14435615R00071